NEW YORK
in Style

A GUIDE TO THE CITY'S FASHION,
DESIGN AND STYLE DESTINATIONS

Dear Helen
Shop till you drop...
+ do a bit of sightseeing x
Love Sheppy
x

MELBOURNE UNIVERSITY PRESS
An imprint of Melbourne University Publishing Limited
11–15 Argyle Place South, Carlton, Victoria 3053, Australia
mup-info@unimelb.edu.au
www.mup.com.au

First published 2014
Text and photography © Janelle McCulloch 2014
Design © Janelle McCulloch 2014

Every attempt has been made to locate the copyright holders for material
quoted in this book. Any person or organisation that may have been
overlooked or misattributed may contact the publisher.

Cover design by Emilia Toia
Typeset by Janelle McCulloch & Bookhouse
Front cover image © Janelle McCulloch
Printed in China by 10/10 Printing Group

National Library of Australia Cataloguing-in-Publication entry

McCulloch, Janelle, author.

New York In Style / Janelle McCulloch

9780522866476 (pbk)

Every care has been taken to ensure the accuracy of the information in this
book. The publisher and author are not able to accept responsibility for any
consequences arising from use of the guide or information it contains. If you do
encounter a factual error, we hope that you will forgive us and let us know, so we
can remedy it for future editions.

Author's website: janellemcculochlibraryofdesign.blogspot.com.au

NY

NEW YORK IN STYLE

New York

Kate Spade's flagship store
on the Upper East Side.

NEW YORK IN STYLE

A GUIDE TO THE CITY'S FASHION, STYLE AND DESIGN DESTINATIONS

WRITTEN AND PHOTOGRAPHED BY
JANELLE McCULLOCH

Kate Spade.
Opposite: Ralph Lauren.

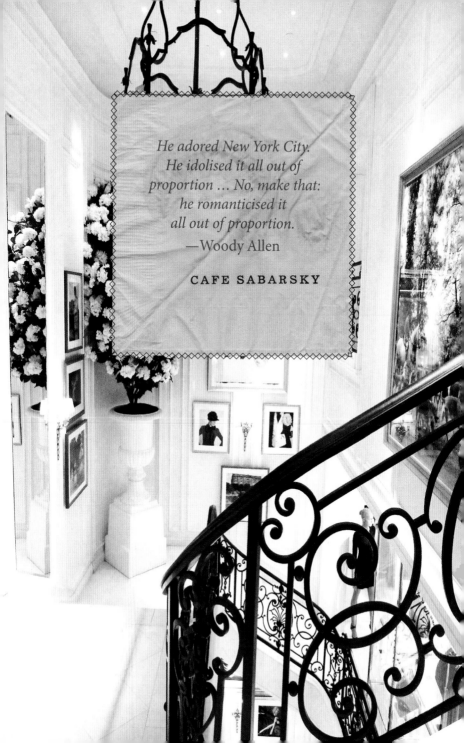

He adored New York City.
He idolised it all out of
proportion ... No, make that:
he romanticised it
all out of proportion.
—Woody Allen

CAFE SABARSKY

OVANDO

Ovando Florist in the West Village.
Opposite: Sephora.

CONTENTS

INTRODUCTION

New York

Over the great bridge … the city rising up across the river in white heaps and sugar lumps all built with a wish … the city seen for the first time, in its first wild promise …
—F. Scott Fitzgerald

Regardless of how you feel about concrete cities and urban insanity, you can't help but feel a frisson of excitement when you arrive in New York City. It is one of the world's most stimulating and exhilarating destinations.

I've been to New York many times, both for business and pleasure, and I'm just as enthralled with it as I was when I first visited as an eight-year-old girl. Every time the taxi drives down the Long Island Expressway and the Chrysler Building comes into view, my heart beats a little faster with expectation. Sometimes I'm even a little emotional. New York's skyline will do that to you.

Unlike Paris, New York doesn't seduce you with its Haussmanian sophistication, its sexy accent, or its French wardrobes and ways. It doesn't have the dignity and grace of London, nor the sunny glamour of Sydney—although it does have its own unique sheen. What it does have, and it has it in spades, is confidence and unending energy. And with that drive and determination New Yorkers have built one of the most incredible destinations in the world.

Not only that, visitors have also been infected with the same zeal. Coming here is like being given a huge vitamin boost. Great surges of energy sweep all around you and the air fizzes like just-opened champagne. The town bubbles over with the promise of life. You feel as though you can do anything; be anyone. Innovative, ambitious, tenacious, creative, iconoclastic, and always, always inspirational, this is a city built on stories and dreams, on tragic failures and

unimaginable successes. Rome may be a poem pressed into service as a city, as the writer Anatole Broyard once put it, but New York is an animated editorial; a brash, page-turner of a tale threaded together with a whole lot of Manhattanesque exclamation marks. Indeed, there are some writers—Woody Allen among them—who spend their entire lives trying to portray this city in print or script. But the fact of the matter is that few superlatives can properly articulate this place, no matter how eloquent. Words alone don't do this place justice. New York is New York. To understand it, you simply have to visit it and experience its distinctive, inimitable style for yourself.

As a journalist, a book editor and an author of eighteen design books, I'm fortunate—and grateful—to have a job that allows me to travel to Manhattan several times a year. After ten years of coming and going from New York, ten years of photographing and writing about its streets, skylines and residences for design books and magazines, I've built up a much-loved (and much-battered) 'black book' of addresses and contacts. Consequently, I'm often asked for the best places to see, shop and stay in New York. In turn, I'm always asking friends, colleagues and work contacts for their suggestions, aware that there is always something new to discover. Even my favourite New York doorman at my favourite New York hotel loves to offer his tips—and graciously refuses to accept a tip of any kind in return.

Perhaps my favourite period in New York was in late 2013, when I travelled to the city to shoot this book.

I love New York, even though
house, something, anyway, that belongs to

It was early September and a lovely late-summer haze had fallen on the city, giving it a golden, almost ethereal glow. Fashion Week was also in full swing, so the streets were hyped with haute glamour. Everywhere you looked models, editors, journalists and other stylish flâneuses seemed to be rushing past, dressed in their sartorial best, just in case *The Sartorialist* or Bill Cunningham walked past. ('We all get dressed for Bill,' *Vogue*'s editor Anna Wintour once said about the legendary *New York Times* photographer.)

As the sun rose bright and unseasonally hot on that first day, warming the sidewalks and sending people to the parks and gelati stands, I decided to walk all the way downtown, to make the most of the urban spectacle. I began from my favourite hotel north of Times Square and headed for Bryant Park, where models were being photographed while New Yorkers looked on in amusement. I then kept walking, taking dozens of photos as I went, down to the Flower District, where I marvelled at one florist bunching pink autumn anemones into huge, blowsy bouquets for a Fashion Week after-party. I continued to the iconic Flatiron Building (a photographer's fave) and then to ABC Carpet & Home where, on a whim, I bought a gorgeous cashmere wrap in a perfect shade of Tiffany blue (very New York).

Then I kept wandering, through Washington Square Park—where a tuxedoed busker was nonchalantly playing Debussy on a shiny black grand piano in the middle of the square—and continued to the Bowery, to shop for curiosities at Paula Rubenstein and John Derian's stores. There I chatted to the well-travelled Ms Rubenstein and found, in John Derian, a vintage, indigo linen French garden smock on sale.

Along the way I saw a gentleman wearing hot-pink linen pants and a citrus lemon blazer with a green parrot sitting on his shoulder, and a woman wearing slim black pants and a fitted, white, tuxedo-style shirt with the most beautiful, enormously puffed out sleeves you've ever seen. Honestly, they were like curtains at the opera, and it was only the tiny black buttons of the cuffs that stopped them blowing off in the breeze.

At the end of the day, after photographing SoHo, I caught a town car back uptown, chauffeured by a driver who normally takes Martha Stewart around. He told me charming anecdotes about Ms Stewart, which enthralled me for the entire ride home.

This is a typical day in New York. You'll never know what you'll see, and you'll never know what you'll discover. It's a city like no other. And its style is one of a kind.

t isn't mine, the way something has to be, a tree or a street or a ne because I belong to it.—Truman Capote

You will no doubt experience your own glorious New York days, remembered with fondness as you board the flight home, trying to hide all those books you've bought from the Strand in your hand luggage. New York never fails to surprise and delight. It may be intimidating and even frustrating (especially at peak hour, in the rain, during taxi driver-changeover time) but it is never, ever boring.

This is of course a highly subjective guidebook, which reflects the personal tastes and insights of its contributors, including this author. You may like or dislike the destinations included. But if, for some reason, you dislike them, don't worry: just walk a block. New York changes so rapidly from neighbourhood to neighbourhood that it's highly likely you'll stumble upon something that will fascinate you, and it's that sort of flâneuring I encourage. New York is full of places and this book cannot hope to cover them all. It is my hope that you will be motivated to explore further and discover some secrets of your own.

I'm so thrilled that you'll have a chance to discover New York for yourself, and I really hope you come away with as many wonderful memories as I have.

Welcome to New York. I hope you'll be inspired.

Janelle McCulloch

MADE IN MANHATTAN

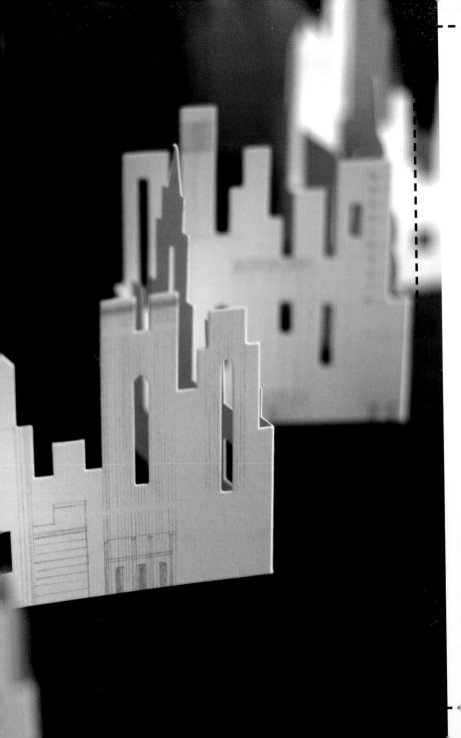

NEW ADDITIONS TO THE NEW YORK LANDSCAPE

Most of this book was written during 2013, and inevitably there have been additions to Manhattan's retail and hotel scene since then. I've included a few of these cute newbies below.

The highly publicised **Club Monaco** store in the Flatiron neighbourhood has been one of the most talked-about spaces since it opened, due to the sublime interior design and the mini bookstore—an offshoot of the famous Strand down the road. The store is sleek and sophisticated: a fitting newcomer for this design quarter. *160 Fifth Avenue. www.clubmonaco.com*

Nearby, the **Hotel Chandler** has recently emerged from a $10m renovation, creating yet another Flatiron fancy to bed down in. *12 East 31st Street. www.hotelchandler.com*

And down in Greenwich Village, The Marlton House has gone through its own makeover, emerging as **The Marlton,** a Parisian-inspired boutique beauty situated near Washington Square Park. It's the work of hotelier Sean MacPherson (The Bowery, the Maritime and the Jane), and the new design is plusher and more feminine than his previous projects. The Marlton's restaurant, **Margaux**, is also great for a casual catch-up with friends. *5 West 8th Street. www.marltonhotel.com*

Kate Spade, meanwhile, has followed the hugely successful launch of its new flagship store on the Upper East Side with a sister store on the Upper West Side. It's small, but extremely stylish. *205 Columbus Avenue. www.katespade.com*

If you're a fan of the **Ladurée** tea salons, you'll be pleased to know that there are now two in New York City. One is on Madison Avenue on the Upper East Side and the second has opened in SoHo. Both have the signature French interiors and exquisite macarons for sale. *396 West Broadway. www.laduree.com*

And while they haven't opened at the time of writing, there are some exciting new hotels coming to town in 2014. **The Archer Hotel** will pay homage to its Garment District location with a mix of fabrics (*6 Times Square; www.archerhotel.com*), the **Knickerbocker Hotel** will re-open to show off its glorious, Beaux Arts architecture, literary links and distinctive mansard roof (*142 West 42nd Street; www.theknickerbocker.com*), and the new **SLS Hotel New York** will open in the now-seriously cool NoMad neighborhood. *444 Park Avenue. www.slshotels.com*

But perhaps the most anticipated newcomer is the luxurious **Baccarat Hotel**, which opens late 2014. Housed in a 45-storey glass tower opposite the MoMA, it's the first US Baccarat Hotel and likely to be as shiny and fine as its sister restaurant in Paris. *20 West 53rd Street. www.baccarathotels.com*

TIPS FROM AN INSIDER

Gary McBournie and Bill Richards
Gary McBournie Inc. Interior Designers
www.gmcbinc.com

PLAZA ATHÉNÉE We're buying an apartment in New York for all the work we do there, but for now this lovely hotel on a charming Upper East Side street is our home away from home. While it's designed to evoke European grandeur, the level of service makes it feel more like a boutique hotel. One of our secrets is to always reserve the same room which provides that extra sense of familiarity. *37 East 64th Street. www.plaza-athenee.com*

BAR ITALIA Sleek, modern and Italian, it's the kind of place where one expects to encounter a sixties-era Sophia and Marcello at a nearby table. I love to slide in at the bar and enjoy the salmon tartare with a glass of crisp white wine. *768 Madison Avenue. www.baritaliamadison.com*

BARNEYS Barneys is a one-stop shop for the gent seeking top style. With all of the major luxury brands represented, this famous retail emporium is a must. We also love to peruse the Home Decor and Accessories department on the 9th floor and meander into **Fred's**, the chic in-store bistro, for a lazy afternoon lunch. *660 Madison Avenue. www.barneys.com*

BERGDORF GOODMAN The window displays at Bergdorfs are some of the best in the world. We love to stroll by late at night and admire both the fantasy and creativity of each vignette. *5th Avenue at 58th Street. www.bergdorfgoodman.com*

BEMELMANS BAR AT THE CARLYLE Classic cocktails, great old standards played on a live piano and murals painted by *Madeleine* author Ludwig Bemelmans evoke Old New York style. *35 East 76th Street. www.rosewoodshotels.com*

TIPS FROM AN INSIDER

India Hicks
Author/designer/ television presenter
Former resident of New York and long-time habituée
www.indiahicks.com

I moved to New York when I was modelling in my early twenties. I lived downtown and I rollerbladed everywhere. Now I return to the city for business. and a tiny bit of pleasure. I no longer know if I belong uptown or downtown so I stay firmly midtown. **The City Club Hotel** is my midtown refuge. Small and discreet with a small team of staff; all with impeccable manners. *55 West 44th Street. www.cityclubhotel.com*

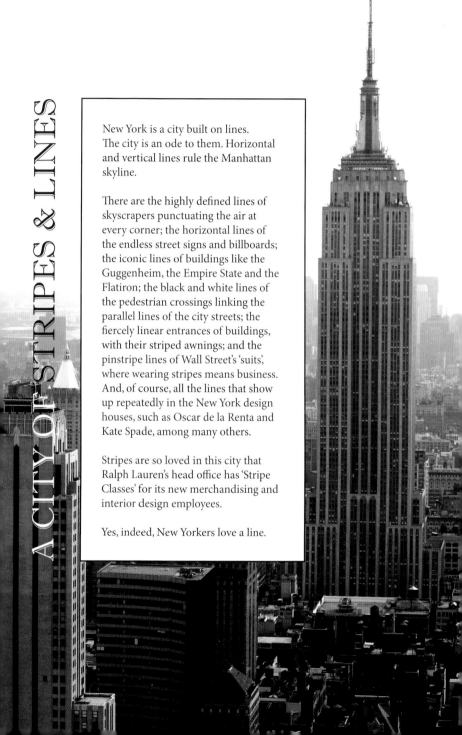

A CITY OF STRIPES & LINES

New York is a city built on lines.
The city is an ode to them. Horizontal
and vertical lines rule the Manhattan
skyline.

There are the highly defined lines of
skyscrapers punctuating the air at
every corner; the horizontal lines of
the endless street signs and billboards;
the iconic lines of buildings like the
Guggenheim, the Empire State and the
Flatiron; the black and white lines of
the pedestrian crossings linking the
parallel lines of the city streets; the
fiercely linear entrances of buildings,
with their striped awnings; and the
pinstripe lines of Wall Street's 'suits',
where wearing stripes means business.
And, of course, all the lines that show
up repeatedly in the New York design
houses, such as Oscar de la Renta and
Kate Spade, among many others.

Stripes are so loved in this city that
Ralph Lauren's head office has 'Stripe
Classes' for its new merchandising and
interior design employees.

Yes, indeed, New Yorkers love a line.

Benoit.
Opposite from top left:
Henri Bendel's book department,
The Guggenheim, a view of the Upper
West Side, and Henri Bendel again.

"One belongs to New York instantly...

One belongs to it as much in five minutes as in five years..."

~ Tom Wolfe

Madison Ave

The Martini glass

Fifth Ave

Stilettos and

Tuxedos

Art Deco

The Empire State

Anna Wintour

Bergdorf's

Black &

White

The martini glass

The triplex penthouse on Fifth Avenue

The annual Met Costume Institute Gala

George Gershwin

Jay Gatsby

The chauffeur-driven black town car

The *New York Times*

Little black dresses and huge heirloom jewellery (often bought at the estate sales at Sotheby's and Christie's)

Fifth Avenue (Saks, The Plaza Hotel, Bergdorf Goodman, Henri Bendel)

Gilded finishes and elegant refinement

The *Wall Street Journal's* glossy magazines

1920s speakeasies and modern mixologists

Fancy summer soirees on rooftop terraces

Sunday walks in Central Park

The films of Woody Allen, Nora Ephron, Martin Scorsese and Mr de Niro

The windows of Bergdorf Goodman

Sex and the City

Stilettos and tuxedos

Black and white stripes

The New York blues

The *New Yorker* (particularly the 'Cut' section of the paper)

The view of New York from atop the Rockefeller Center (particularly at twilight when the sun sets over the Empire State Building and the city looks like the ending credits in a film)

Art Deco architecture

Fashion, *Vogue* and Anna Wintour

Bold fonts—and bolder business ideas

The Empire State Building

The Chrysler Building

Cecil Beaton, Grace Coddington, Bill Cunningham and all the other creatives inspired by New York's fine lines

Browsing vintage books at the Strand bookstore—and seeing a rare copy of Grace Coddington's first book among the shelves | Finding the perfect designer shoes in your size in the sales at Saks Fifth Avenue | Having lunch in the sun at the Shake Shack | Walking through the cherry blossoms in the Conservatory Gardens on a spring morning | Eating brunch beneath porcelain dinner-plate displays and chic lemon-yellow walls at Caffé Storico | Stumbling across a vintage Dior necklace at the antique markets on West 26th Street | Meeting a friend for pre-dinner drinks at NoMad Hotel's Library Bar, or late-night drinks at the Library Hotel's rooftop bar | Catching a fashion exhibition at the Met | Buying some peonies in the Flower District—and then some Ralph Lauren remnant fabric to match at Mood in the Garment District | Gazing at the architecture along the High Line | Grabbing lunch at the Union Square Greenmarket, followed by a wander through Washington Mews and the park | Watching an outdoor movie in Bryant Park on a summer's night | Bicycling along the Hudson River on a sunny weekend | Having a late lunch on the rooftop of Gramercy Park Hotel or Balthazar Restaurant | Accepting a romantic date at Eleven Madison Park restaurant | Planning for a weekend away in Montauk | Looking forward to returning to New York and doing everything all over again …

24 (STYLISH) HOURS IN NY

Book a room at the pretty, Parisian-style NoMad Hotel on West 28th Street, just north of Madison. It's the hottest hotel in New York right now, and possibly for the next ten years—it's that beautiful. (Tip: Reserve one of the rooms with the claw-foot bathtubs, because you'll need it after you follow my itinerary below.)

If you're early, leave your bags with the charming doormen and have a peek at the Parlour, the Atrium and the much-touted Library Bar (a cocktail here later will be lovely), then head straight out to the Antiques Markets on West 26th to find some vintage 1920s Chanel or Dior jewellery. With bijoux in hand(bag), saunter down to Madison Square Park and grab a coffee at the Shake Shack while admiring the Flatiron's famously sharp cheese-grater lines. Wander the nabe around East 20th Street (great shopping at Kate Spade, ABC Carpet & Home and Fishs Eddy), then refuel with a smoothie at the atmospheric Union Square Greenmarket (Mondays, Wednesdays, Fridays, Saturdays).

Walk a few blocks south to the Strand Bookstore, sole survivor of New York's old Book Row, for a browse through the vintage fashion and design books (including the rare ones on the top floor). Then walk a few more blocks south to East 2nd Street, to John Derian's cluster of retail whimsy. Walk due west along Bond Street for more sublime shops (Paula Rubenstein's vintage emporium is a must).

Then skip SoHo's crowded madness (although detour via Elizabeth Street if you want, as there are some gorgeous stores there, too), and instead keep those feet walking west along Bleecker Street for some more retail glamour. Follow Bleecker all the way up to the West Village (think of the workout!), where you'll be rewarded with more sumptuous stuff, including Marc Jacobs' Bookmarc—great for design titles. Along the way, look out for Maison Martin Margiela, Michael Kors, Isabel Marant and Ovando florist (the most beautiful in Manhattan), along with pop-up stores that appear, like that from Karl Lagerfeld. It's a lot of style for a little 'hood.

Feet weary? Then grab a taxi uptown to NoMad and change into your va-va-voom best for dinner at Eleven Madison, where the dishes and presentation are so surprising and original that foodies write home about them (reservations are advised). The best thing is, you can walk there and back from the hotel. Easy. Then finish the day with a cheeky nightcap at either the Ace Hotel, the Breslin or NoMad's own Library Bar. Bliss.

In the morning, check out, leave your bags at the hotel and grab coffee at Stumptown (inside the Ace Hotel), then walk a few blocks north to the bucolic Bryant Park. Pause. Breathe in the beauty. Some optional stops on Fifth Avenue include Top of the Rock for sublime views of the Empire and Central Park, Henri Bendel (lovely gifts on the second floor at the rear), Bergdorf Goodman or Assouline inside the Plaza Hotel for stylish new reads. Continue up to Central Park for some fresh air and horticultural loveliness before heading back to the hotel by taxi to grab your bags, tired but happy. Congrats: you've packed a lot of New York into a little day.

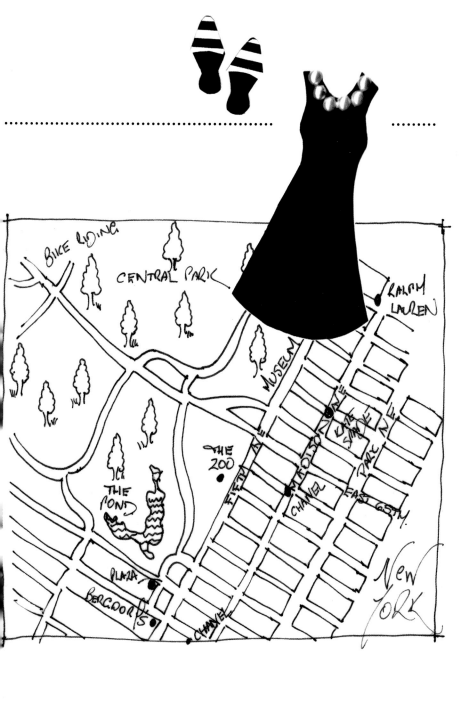

NEW YORK MUST SEES

A hundred times have I thought New York is a catastrophe,
and fifty times: It is a beautiful catastrophe.—Le Corbusier

A SECOND CHANCE Possibly one of the best stores in New York, this tiny, tucked-away boutique on the Upper East Side sells—wait for this—authentic Chanel pieces for amazing prices. There are two stores but the one on the UES is dedicated to couture. It's re-sale Chanel, of course, but it all comes from wealthy socialites, so much of it is either from recent collections or in good condition. They also stock Chanel jewellery and coats from the likes of YSL and Prada. The last time I popped in, there were Hermès bags and Chanel dresses on sale. And it's all guaranteed to be authentic, with a 100% money-back guarantee. *1111 Lexington Avenue. www.asecondchanceresale.com*

ARCHTOBER A chance to see New York up close, this festival is run in October by the American Institute of Architects New York Chapter and the Center for Architecture. It offers more than 150 programs, including exhibits, movies, talks and walking tours by leading architects and design professionals. *www.archtober.org*

BERGDORF GOODMAN One of the most beautiful department stores in the world, Bergdorfs always carries luxurious product lines that are a little different from other stores. And the window merchandising is so famous there is even a book about it! The Kelly Wearstler–designed BG Restaurant on the seventh floor has eye-popping views over Fifth Avenue's rooftop gardens, penthouses and the treetops of Central Park. It's a favourite with Fifth Avenue socialites. Sit back and try not to gawp with surprise when you overhear the gossip. *Fifth Avenue at 58th Street. www.bergdorfgoodman.com*

BRYANT PARK FILM FESTIVAL A wonderful, quintessential New York experience, Bryant Park's film nights are a must-do in summer. There's nothing like watching a classic movie under the night sky amid the greenery of this gorgeous park. *Bryant Park (near 40th Street and Fifth Avenue). www.bryantpark.org*

THE COSTUME INSTITUTE AT THE METROPOLITAN MUSEUM OF ART The exhibitions held here are some of the most well curated in the world. (Diana Vreeland's legacy clearly lives on.) And while you're at the Met, don't miss the American Wing, with its architectural facades and historic interiors; it beautifully narrates the story of American domestic architecture and furnishings. *1000 Fifth Avenue. www.metmuseum.org*

FLATIRON DISTRICT The Flatiron District has come of age in the last year or so. It was always an interesting part of town, with the Flatiron Building, Gramercy Park

and other intriguing landmarks. However, there were too few great hotels and even fewer great places to eat. In the last few years though, it's become a real Manhattan 'hot-spot' with the arrival of the Ace Hotel, the new NoMad and Chandler hotels, Eleven Madison Park restaurant, new Marimekko and Club Monaco stores (the latter has an outpost of the Strand bookstore), and of course perennial favourites like the Shake Shack. If you only have time to explore a few neighbourhoods in New York, make this one of them.

FLOWER DISTRICT A scented street that smells as good as it looks. It doesn't matter which florist you go into on West 28th Street, they will all reward you with huge, blowsy bunches of fragrant pleasure. My favourite is New York Topiary, where it seems that every single plant imaginable has been trained into exquisite shapes—an absolute joy to explore. *135 West 28th Street. www.nytopiary.com*

HIGH LINE This is a mile-long New York park built in a highly unusual manner, elevated above the city rather than at ground level. You may think an old railway line would be boring, but the High Line is an extraordinary combination of superb horticultural displays, urban pleasure and leisure zones (think chic timber deckchairs upon which to read in the sun) and head-turning vistas of New York's architecture and streets. Join the throng and embrace the atmosphere. *Gansevoort Street in the Meatpacking District to West 34th Street, between 10th and 11th Avenues. www.thehighline.org*

INA Ina's stores are quite possibly the best high-end fashion boutiques in New York. There are several locations, and each sells everything from Lanvin to Hermès and gently used Louboutin heels at half the normal price. Junior fashion editors come here to supplement their wardrobes, and even senior ones have been known to browse the rails. Stylists love it. There are so many highly covetable bags you're liable to get a sartorial version of Stendhal's syndrome looking through them all. *SoHo, Nolita and Chelsea locations. www.inanyc.com*

JAZZ AGE LAWN PARTY ON GOVERNORS ISLAND For the past eight years, this wonderful event has been persuading New Yorkers to kick up their heels. It encourages people to get decked out in 1920s gear and catch the ferry to Governors Island, where they are transported to an era of flappers, jazz and general prohibition madness. There are authentic old gramophones playing original records from the 1920s, dance lessons, vintage portraits, a 1920s motorcar exhibition and a Charleston dance contest—all for only a US$30 ticket. The event occurs twice over the summer, but

dates can vary, so see the website for details. *Governors Island. www.jazzagelawnparty.com*

JOHN DERIAN Curated by collector John Derian, these stores are an intriguing triptych of boutiques offering some of the most fascinating products in Manhattan. Although he's mostly famous for his deliciously pretty decoupage trays and paperweights, Derian has also diversified into all kinds of lovely stuff—beautifully coloured textiles, covetable furniture with a hint of vintage and even garden pieces. These boutiques are always full of browsers and it's easy to see why. *6, 8 and 10 East 2nd Street (three stores). www.johnderian.com*

KATE SPADE Kate Spade's new flagship store features a whimsically pretty, cocktail-coloured, 1950s-style interior that feels like an elegant townhouse. Go and see it just for the décor and furniture. And okay, the clothes too. Truly charming. *789 Madison Avenue. www.katespade.com*

MOOD FABRICS This is an enormous, three-storey store devoted entirely to haberdashery. There are aisles and aisles of beautiful bolts but the best ones are the leftover fabric remnants from the collections of Ralph Lauren, Carolina Herrera, Marc Jacobs, Oscar de la Renta, Vera Wang, Calvin Klein and Donna Karan. *225 West 37th Street. www.moodfabrics.com*

NANCY BRYAN LUCE HERB GARDEN AND PEGGY ROCKEFELLER ROSE GARDEN AT THE NEW YORK BOTANICAL GARDENS The New York Botanical Gardens is truly an enchanting garden space. With a 50-acre forest, a stunning conservatory, a perennial garden and much more, it's certainly worth the trek uptown. But it's the Nancy Bryan Luce Herb Garden that everyone's talking about. With 150 varieties of herbs set within a glorious formal boxwood parterre, it makes for a serene—and scented—escape from the madness of Manhattan. The Peggy Rockefeller Rose Garden, with its 2700 varieties of roses, is one of the loveliest places to be in the city on an early summer's morning. *2900 Southern Boulevard. www.nybg.org*

NEW YORK PUBLIC LIBRARY A beautiful building that backs onto the equally beautiful Bryant Park. If you love books, this is a must-see. The Rose Main

Reading Room is astonishingly elegant while the soaring entrance hall, where Carrie was famously dumped at her wedding to Mr Big, is surely the most handsome entrance in the whole of Manhattan. *Fifth Avenue at 42nd Street. www.nypl.org*

OPEN HOUSE NEW YORK This annual weekend celebrating the city's architecture and design allows design lovers to tour buildings not normally open to the general public. From private residences and historic landmarks to rooftop gardens and the tops of skyscrapers, this event offers rare access into the extraordinary architecture that defines New York. *www.ohny.org*

ROSEN & CHADICK My newest discovery in the Garment District, this store is a more upmarket version of Mood Fabrics. It's tricky to find, but you'll love it when you do: the double-level store is filled with high-end fabrics, including many remnant fabrics from designers such as Armani, who sell them when they've finished designing their collections. It stocks 125 linen colours alone. Leave plenty of time; you'll stay much longer than you intended to. *561 7th Avenue. www.rosenandchadickfabrics.com*

VINTAGE DEPARTMENT OF THE STRAND BOOKSTORE The iconic Strand bookstore is where you're liable to find all kinds of literary treasures—including great fashion and design books. The ground and first floors are dazzling departments; the kinds of places where you promise yourself you won't buy anything but then find yourself, two hours later, wondering if you need to get a taxi home. However, it's when you reach the top floor that real desire sets in. There are thousands of vintage books here, including highly covetable fashion tomes that sell for a fortune on Amazon. There are $1 stalls outside too—book-buying bliss. *828 Broadway. www.strandbooks.com*

WEST VILLAGE A true village (complete with doll's house homes and cobbled lanes) that's devoid of skyscrapers and noise. In the last few years some of the more eclectic stores have moved out, after the place grew popular and the rents soared, but there's still a lot of character left in the neighbourhood. Shopping is good too, as is the dining scene. *Between Hudson River and Seventh Avenue.*

CLASS
is in
session.

Clockwise from top left: Bergdorf
Goodman, vintage Chanel in the Bowery,
a mirrored window display in the West
Village and Kate Spade.

Opposite: The New York Public Library,
The Metropolitan Museum of Art
and John Derian's fabrics and furniture.

PRACTICALITIES

BEST TIMES TO VISIT

Every season in New York has its own appeal, and its own charm. If you have children, **November and December** are wonderful months to go: the Christmas tree at the Rockefeller Centre is up, the skating rink beneath it is full of people (as is the one in Central Park), most stores go all out to display staggeringly beautiful Christmas windows and there is a real sparkle in the streets. It's New York as you've always imagined it. The kids will adore it.

However, the spring months are also splendid. **Late April and May** is particularly sublime because the spring bulbs are out in the street gardens and kerb-side flower beds and the crab apples and other blossom trees in Central Park, particularly the Conservatory Gardens, make for a spectacular sight. It's one of the prettiest times to be here.

Even New Yorkers seem to become a little more animated when spring kicks in.

Autumn (or fall), in **September and October** is also gorgeous; the leaves are changing colour in Central Park and—as with spring—people seem to be revived by the cooler days after suffering the long, languid months of summer. New York comes alive again; there is a sense of optimism in the air.

The only time to perhaps avoid New York is **summer.** The city can be hot, windy and unpleasant during the months of **July and August,** when the heat settles in the concrete canyons of Manhattan and the dry wind blows an urban version of hell up Fifth Avenue. Summer is when many New Yorkers escape the city for the beaches or the cool hills of the country. A few days in town and you'll be ready to join them!

TRAVEL TIP:
Don't take a taxi from the airport—
unless it's late at night or you have lots
of luggage. If it's daytime, opt for the
New York Airport Service Express Bus
(*$15; www.nyairportservice.com*), which
connects the three major airports to
central Manhattan via Grand Central,
Port Authority and Penn Station. Or
catch the AirTrain that connects to the
New York subway. *www.airtrainjfk.com*

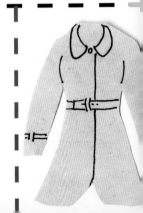

NAVIGATING NY
(with ease)

WALKING

The best way to see New York is to walk. It allows you to discover streets and sights you might otherwise miss in a cab or train. It's also quicker than a taxi or the subway in many cases, especially in peak hour. And it's a great workout. How you do think the locals get so thin? Each block is relatively small, so you can cover a good distance in a short amount of time. Pack some fabric Band-Aids and some comfy flats, and you'll be all set. The best thing to do is to buy a small map of the city from any of the bookstores or street vendors that sell newspapers and magazines and keep it in your handbag.

The only problem with walking is, your feet can become weary, especially if your shoes aren't designed for pounding the streets. I tend to keep an eye out for my favourite flat shoe stores. I can't tell you the number of times I've had to make a detour to Aerosoles on Fifth Avenue. Their loafers may not be Manolos but they are decent designs and when they save your feet from being torn to blistery shreds as you're racing around, you'll be grateful.

TAXIS

If you get really weary from walking and can't face the subway, simply hail a taxi. Taxi fares are very cheap in this city—$10–20 will usually get you a fair way from downtown to uptown or visa versa—but do tip: 15 per cent is standard. Here's another trick: stand on a street where the taxis are going in your direction. Many of New York's streets are one-way and it's no good standing on a street where all the cars are flowing downtown if you're heading north. Simply walk across to a parallel street where the cars are driving in your direction.

TOWN CARS

If you have the cash and want to see New York quickly, grab a town car. A town car is a particularly great idea if you have a party of three and want to make the most of your time—or want to cover broad areas in one day. It's also a good idea if you want to go out of town for the day, perhaps to the Hamptons or Connecticut. It saves organising a rental car and battling the traffic, and the vehicles are always luxurious.

start here

SHOPPING

Many people I know go to New York for one thing: shopping. The sales are usually in June/July and late December/early January, and they're incredible. (Note: many shops have now started discounting before Christmas, to improve retail sales, rather than waiting until Boxing Day.) But even outside of the sales I've picked up J. Crew trench coats for $5 and stunning leather handbags for $10. Cosmetics are a good buy, too: I always try to stock up on MAC, which is cheaper than in Australia and Europe.

As for books, well New York is a booklover's dream. Just try resisting the cheap titles in the Strand or any of the other great bookstores. You'll soon be buying an extra suitcase to bring everything home. (Tip: Don't take much to New York to begin with, or pack a small suitcase inside a larger one to accommodate both your everyday clothes and all the loot you'll buy there.)

Other great buys include fabrics (amazing remnants from the likes of Armani, Diane von Furstenberg and Ralph Lauren can be found in the Garment District), homewares and interior design pieces (Dash and Albert, and Madeline Weinrib rugs are cheaper here, and the latter always has a garage sale in May and September), and of course shoes and handbags. Lots of antiques and vintage whimsy in the streets around the Flatiron, too.

SHIPPING

If you buy so much that you can't fit everything into your airline's luggage allowance, the best thing is to post it home.

There are USP (post) offices all over New York. They also have boxes, tape and anything else you need. (Tip: ensure you take out any really valuable things, or hard-edged purchases and take those on the plane with you. Just send clothes and soft items home. It won't matter if they get creased and customs tend not to bother checking clothes.)

Fedex is also good and there are many outlets all over Manhattan, with most open 24 hours. So if you're desperate the night before you fly it's a good last-minute resort. However, it is the more expensive option.

Otherwise, if you have frequent flyer membership with your airline, you can try your luck with overweight luggage. United Airlines once let me sneak 60 kilos of books through, as I was a frequent flyer. But I wouldn't count on the airlines to do this all the time!

The Sherry Netherland.
Opposite: The NoMad Hotel.

HOTELS AND DINING

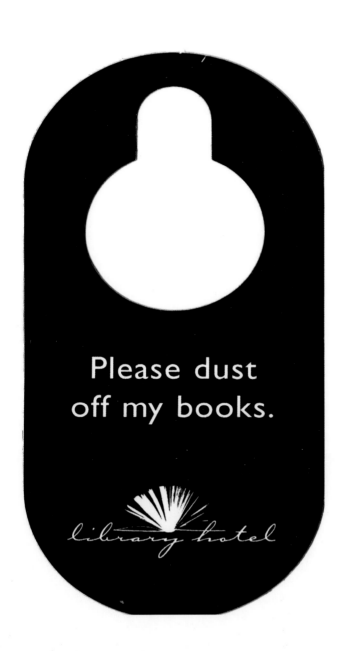

Please dust
off my books.

library hotel

TIPS FOR FINDING PLACES TO STAY

Okay, let's get the bad news out of the way: New York hotels are some of the most expensive in the world. If you want a decent room, you won't get much change out of US$300+ a night. Now multiply that by seven for a week's stay, and then add the various taxes (approximately 15% of the bill, on top of your bill), and you can see why New York is a killer city to sleep in. Thankfully, there are ways to stay in New York without sinking into a hefty debt.

BOOK YOUR STAY TO COINCIDE WITH A WEEKEND New York hotels are often considerably cheaper on weekends because business executives and their expense accounts aren't around to fill rooms.

BOOK A SUNDAY Sunday night is cheaper still—usually half the price of weekdays.

BOOK A SMALLER, LESSER-KNOWN BOUTIQUE HOTEL RATHER THAN A COOL NAME OR A SWANKY BRAND Hotels such as The Mercer, Crosby Street, Gramercy Park, The Mark and The Surrey are always going to be expensive because their global reputations mean they're always sure of premium-paying guests. If you can do without the cool factor, there are lovely little hideaways tucked in between the swanky brands. Try the Roger New York (stylish navy interior with a cute bow tie as its motif and surprisingly spacious rooms), or the Night Hotel near Times Square (seductively dark with a sexy, Gotham Cityesque aesthetic, but rooms can be compact). There are lots more—see my list in this section.

BOOK AN APARTMENT If you're in New York for longer than three days or are travelling with one or two others, it may be cheaper to book an apartment. Airbnb, a leading agency in apartment rentals, has recently come under scrutiny, particularly in New York, where the council is cracking down on anybody subletting their place to tourists, but there are other agencies, such as onefinestay, that offer gorgeous and roomy places.

BOOK YOUR ACCOMMODATION THROUGH AN ONLINE AGENCY These include sites such as Tablet Hotels (*www.tablethotels.com*), Booking.com or Priceline.com. Quite often these sites will offer good deals. Once I found a room at the normally expensive Gramercy Park Hotel for half the standard rate via Booking.com. Tablet Hotels will also often offer a free upgrade upon arrival.

TRY YOUR LUCK AND ASK THE RECEPTION DESK FOR A 'WALK-UP RATE' This will often be a very good deal; far lower than the standard 'rack rate'. I once arrived in New York without accommodation and asked a hotel for a walk-up rate: they offered me a suite for just $199 a night as opposed to $950 a night, simply because it was late and they wanted my business.

LOOK FOR HOTELS THAT ARE OPENING UP Hotel openings are usually timed for April/May or September/October, so check sites such as hotelchatter.com to see which openings are coming up. These places will almost always do a 'soft opening' a few weeks before their 'official opening' and will offer a hugely discounted rate for this period, while work is still being done.

ROOMS FOR A ROMANTIC WEEKEND

THE BOWERY HOTEL This is a much-loved home-away-from-home for design lovers, who adore its marble soaking baths and cute bistro. The Lower East Side neighbourhood is beloved by some, bypassed by others, but it's slowly becoming a haven for design stores, so gentrification isn't far off. *335 Bowery. www.theboweryhotel.com*

CITY CLUB HOTEL There's nothing else like the suites of the City Club, anywhere in New York. Carved out of a former ballroom, the hotel's three duplexes have their own libraries, but the ornate, double-height ceilings and Palladian windows are the real reason most design lovers check in here. That and the fab location near Bryant Park. *55 West 44th Street. www.cityclubhotel.com*

GRAMERCY PARK HOTEL Still pulling in the VIP names, the GPH is a dramatic, theatrical and utterly divine place to stay. The rooms are heavenly, and the rooftop terrace restaurant is fab for brunch, but it's the key to the exclusive greenery of Gramercy Park that is the real appeal for many guests. *2 Lexington Avenue. www.gramercyparkhotel.com*

LIBRARY HOTEL Book lovers go mad for the Library, which is modelled after a real library, complete with bookshelves in the lobby and the stylish upstairs bar. (It's also near the NY Public Library.) Rooms are named subjects, complete with Dewey decimal codes, and feature books of the same genre. Some of the rooms can be small, so splurge and go for an upgrade. The rooftop bar is always buzzing, too. *299 Madison Avenue. www.libraryhotel.com*

HOTELS FOR FASHION AND DESIGN LOVERS

...WBIES

HIGH L... HOTEL This little-known hotel is a serene retreat in the Meatpacking District created from the cloistered shell of a seminary by the clever boys who did the super-hip Ace Hotel. The design has a Ralph Lauren look, only more austere and surprisingly pleasing. *180 10th Avenue. www.thehighlinehotel.com*

HOTEL CHANDLER Joining the throng of new places choosing to make the Flatiron neighbourhood their home, the Hotel Chandler is a boutique beauty with a quiet but elegant design and a stirling location. One for people who don't like lots of fuss—in design or otherwise. *12 East 31st Street. www.hotelchandler.com*

NOMAD HOTEL The NoMad is a fancy, schmanzy, Parisian-inspired glamourpuss designed by Jacques Garcia that's helping to revive the NoMad/Flatiron neighbourhood. Don't miss the hotel's handsome Library Bar for pre-dinner drinks, the pretty Atrium or plush Parlour for dinner, then the view of the lights of the Empire State Building from the showstopper rooftop, with its restored copper cupola. One of the most beautiful hotels in Manhattan. *1170 Broadway. www. thenomadhotel.com*

REFINERY HOTEL New fashion lover's hideaway in the heart of the Garment District. Created from a former millinery factory, it's now as sleek as a Martin Margiela number. *63 West 38th Street. www.refineryhotelnewyork.com*

THE JADE HOTEL Sexy, somewhat secret, 1920s-style boîte in downtown Greenwich Village. It has a slight French Deco look and a seductively dark bistro out back

that's made for a romantic rendezvous. Bijoux but beautiful. *52 West 13th Street. www.thejadenyc.com*

THE MARLTON The subject of much recent media, The Marlton is a little gem of a place tucked away in Greenwich Village. It's known for its literary connections (Jack Kerouac penned a book here), but the new design will win new fans. Rooms are small but adorable, while the restaurant is a sublime slice of loveliness. *5 West 8th Street. www.marltonhotel.com*

HOTELS FOR WHEN SOMEONE ELSE IS PAYING

THE MARK Posh uptown spot loved by the affluent crowd. Lavish rooms, and the bar's always good for people watching. *25 East 77th Street. www.themarkhotel.com*

THE PLAZA HOTEL A New York classic, still going strong after all these years. The luxe interior is worth a look even if you're not staying the night. The location—bang between Bergdorf Goodman and Central Park—is surely the best in town. *768 Fifth Avenue. www.theplazany.com*

THE SURREY As sophisticated as can be (not surprisingly, considering the Upper East Side location). Inspired by Coco's motifs (beige, quilting, gilt), it's a frankly swanky ode to style. The Chanelesque bar is particularly chic. Chanel would have been proud. *20 East 76th Street. www.thesurrey.com*

INEXPENSIVE DIGS THAT STILL OFFER A DECENT DESIGN

NIGHT HOTELS Black and white beauty tucked midtown between Times Square and Fifth/Sixth shopping areas. Part modern Gothic and part glamour. May be too dark and seductive for some, but for others it's location and luxe in one. *132 West 45th Street. www.nighthotels.com*

GILD HALL Another glammed-up boarding school–style hideaway with a lovely library and Ralph Lauren–style rooms. It's in FiDi (the Financial District) and may be too out of the way for some, but for others this is becoming a hot new neighbourhood. Often offers great rates through Tablet Hotels. *15 Gold Street. www.thompsonhotels.com*

ROGER NEW YORK Pretty, newly renovated gem on Madison Avenue, with smart navy interiors, a whimsical bow tie motif and a truly gorgeous foyer (with petrol-blue chesterfield sofas and black-and-white photos), plus affordable suites with enormous outdoor terraces—virtually unheard of in Manhattan. *131 Madison Avenue. www.therogernewyork.com*

HOTELS FOR PURE ENTERTAINMENT

ACE HOTEL A Bohemian's dream and one of the first to do the industrial-loft-meets-boys'-boarding-school look. Rooms can be slightly austere but the fun's downstairs anyway. The lobby is so cool passers-by use it to chill out. Always buzzing. *20 West 29th Street. www.acehotel.com*

THE EMPIRE HOTEL Super-glam and super-huge, but hasn't lost its personal touch. Made famous by regular appearances in *Gossip Girl*. The leopard-print and tangerine lobby is surprisingly chic. Ed's Chowder House downstairs is a fave of celebs and fashion peeps, perhaps because it's close to Fashion Week shows at the Lincoln Centre. *44 West 63rd Street. www.empirehotelnyc.com*

THE GREENWICH HOTEL Robert de Niro's hotel and restaurant continue to be as much of a hit as his films. *377 Greenwich Street. www.thegreenwichhotel.com*

THE MERCER Sleekly minimalist SoHo hideaway that's still booked solid by the celebrity set. The bookshelf-lined lobby and restaurant are always full of people having power lunches to carve out their next literary/movie deal. *147 Mercer Street. www.mercerhotel.com*

SOHO HOUSE NEW YORK The Manhattan outpost of the hugely popular London-based hotel group. The rooftop pool was immortalised in a *Sex and the City* episode. Like all of the Soho properties, the interior has a British country house feel, but this one feels as though it's been bred with a New York loft apartment. *29–35 9th Avenue. www.sohouseny.com*

APARTMENTS TO RENT

AIRBNB This site has been a popular alternative to hotels for the past few years, but please note that local governments and councils are cracking down on Airbnb and the apartment owners themselves, particularly in New York, where it seems to go against local laws, so research well before you venture into this. Some people love Airbnb; others are dubious. As I said, just research it well and you'll make up your own mind. *www.airbnb.com*

ONEFINESTAY Another great alternative to pricey hotels, onefinestay's apartments and homes are all high-end residences. I have heard nothing but great things about this company. One of their properties, a duplex carriage house in Manhattan, looks divine. And unlike some of the entries on Airbnb, where you can only rent the room, onefinestay offers you the entire apartment or home to rent for the week. *www.onefinestay.com*

CROSBY STREET HOTEL
A colour-infused, design delight in downtown SoHo that's particularly adored by interior designers. It's one of co-owner Kit Kemp's best hotel projects. If you can afford it, opt for the suites (pictured). The rooftop kitchen garden is a great touch.
79 Crosby Street. www.firmdalehotels.com

Gramercy Park Hotel.
Opposite: The Crosby Street Hotel.

The NoMad Hotel.
Opposite: Balthazar.

Beautiful Bistros,
Restaurants and Bars

TIPS FROM AN INSIDER

Paula Perlini
Paula Perlini Interior Design
www.paulaperlini.com

My favorite restaurant in NY is called **El Rio Grande**. It's a terrific Mexican restaurant with outside seating area in the summer, large windows all around and crazy Mexican decorations. It's really good fun food and has fantastic margaritas! I've gone there for years and still love it. The waiters and staff are wonderful and it always feels like a party. *160 East 38th Street. www.elriograndenyc.com*

BACK ROOM Accessed via a secret alley and staircase (the entrance is marked by a sign that says 'Lower East Side Toy Company': very witty considering the playthings inside), this is a classic speakeasy that's packing debaucherous New Yorkers into its dim corners. (If there's no bouncer and the door is closed, just knock and wait: one will eventually let you in. If they sneer, give them some attitude back.) It's an extraordinary space that transports you back to the 1920s, with a live band playing jazz and a wet bar that serves hard-liquor drinks in teacups and beers in brown paper bags. But don't let the drinking vessels fool you: the gilded interior and elegant overhead chandeliers will make you feel as though you're living the good life in prohibition times. *102 Norfolk Street. www.backroom.nyc.com*

BALTHAZAR Still a firm favourite with New Yorkers, even after all these years. Keith McNally's beguiling Parisian-style brasserie could just about show the French how restaurant design is done. The interior is beautiful, and the food is even better. The steak frites are a staple but other dishes, such as a dessert of fig with vanilla sabayon, are incredible. And the conversations are similarly memorable. I once sat next to an investment banker at the bar (if there are no tables available, it's a great spot to eat) and we had a two-hour discussion about Brooklyn, politics and travel. I tell you, Balthazar is always a good time. The only problem is the waiting time for a table: the only way around the queue is to book in advance or go at an earlier or later hour. *80 Spring Street. www.balthazarny.com*

```
Balthazar Bar
80 Spring Street, NYC
(212) 965-1414

301 AM          WIEDERMARK
CHK 4504   JUN07'12   1:32PM

1 LAMB SAND
1 DIET
Subtotal
Tax                    $22
Amount Due
Le BALTHAZAR COOK
```

BAR NANÁ This bar in MePa (the Meatpacking District) is the go-to spot for many movers and shakers of the fashion industry. It may have a cute name but the cocktails are a killer. It's a hot late-night spot where the swirl of models and hangers-on can make you heady at times, but it's uncertain whether it will still be jumping in a year or so. Probably, but we'll see. *63 Gansevoort Street. www.barnananyc.com*

BEATRICE INN *Vanity Fair's* editor-in-chief, Graydon Carter, is one of the names behind the West Village's Beatrice Inn, so you know it's going to be a hangout for beautiful people. The building, which dates back to 1840, has been beautifully restored without losing its integrity or charm—the New York Times described the refit as 'handsome', and indeed it is. And with former Per Se sous chef Brian Nasworthy behind the outstanding menu (modern American fare at its best), you know it's going to be dine-worthy. *285 West 12th Street. www.thebeatriceinn.com*

BENOIT The first sign that you're entering somewhere memorable is the graphic black-and-white bar: a startling, high-glam affair that feels distinctly Parisian. It leads to an equally stylish restaurant that's also reminiscent of a 100-year-old French bistro. Very Montmartre-in-Manhattan. It's the concept of Alain Ducasse, who wanted a New York outpost of his Paris bistro, and—like any Ducasse project—it's been a hit since it opened. André Leon Talley loves it. So do a lot of the fashion crowd, who come here for Fashion Week after-parties. *60 West 55th Street. www.benoitny.com*

BILL'S For many years, this prohibition-style bar had a legion of loyal (drinking) fans. Whiskey was the drink du jour (or du noir), while a pianist banged out the classics. But then it changed hands and its regulars fretted it would end up as just another slick, cookie-cutter bar with no soul and skyscraper-priced drinks. Well, thankfully the new Bill's has atmosphere in spades—or should that be ice buckets. The walls have been redone and a dazzling array of gilded mirrors and framed paintings now set the scene: it's still as nostalgic as the old Bill's but now the look is bright, cheery, kick-up-your-heels, F. Scott Fitzgerald-ish, rather than Hemingway-sagged-over-in-a-cloud-of-cigar-smoke. The food is also very Fitzgerald, with caviar going for $110. You have been warned. *57 East 54th Street. www.bills54.com*

BOOKMARKS LOUNGE AT THE LIBRARY HOTEL Bookish beauties love this place, and its popularity isn't surprising. There are few places in New York (yes, even New York) where you can take the lift to a penthouse-on-the-rooftop-style hideaway and then bunker down next to a roaring fire with a good book and a fine wine. Maybe in a private residence, but a public bar? The Peninsula is the only other one I know of and that doesn't have the same library-style feel as this. It's one of the best places to meet literary-minded friends, with cosy sofas and club chairs, an enclosed greenhouse and an outdoor terrace—the ideal perch for sipping drinks in summer and gazing out at Manhattan. *299 Madison Avenue. www.libraryhotel.com*

CAFÉ CLUNY Café Cluny is so pretty that even uptowners trek all the way down here for weekend brunch. It's classic West Village: chic with a cool twist. The walls are peppered with naturalist displays (green pressed fern fronds under glass in one corner; electric-blue butterfly display in another corner), and staff bustle about dressed in navy-and-white striped Breton T-shirts and long linen aprons, delivering menus with a faint whiff of French flavour. (The roast chicken is particularly delish.) Even the street outside is cobblestoned to fit the theme. Not surprisingly, the place was

inspired by France (the name comes from Abbaye de Cluny monastery), but there's no French pretension here. Just good food delivered with prompt New York service. *284 West 12th Street. www.cafecluny.com*

THE FAT RADISH Like its name, the loft-like Fat Radish is a simple space, but it gives off a whole lotta confidence—just like its patrons. (In fact, the clientele here look like they've just finished work on a catwalk. And don't get me started on the waiters.) A former sausage factory, it's now a hip hangout for art directors, magazine writers, models, photographers and other creatives who love the interior design—including the old plaster and hand-lettered signs that can still be seen on the bare brick walls. The rustic, gastro-pub menu may be inspired by Great Britain but the space is pure New York. *17 Orchard Street. www.thefatradishnyc.com*

FREEMANS Part bar, part taxidermy museum, part speakeasy, this spot isn't so secret anymore, but it's still a great discovery. Filled with beautiful people dressed in their edgiest New York best, it's a darkly atmospheric bar and restaurant with a fascinating turn-of-the-century feel. It's difficult to find (keep going down the dead-end alley) but it's an experience when you get there. *191 Chrystie Street. www.freemansrestaurant.com*

NOMAD HOTEL This utterly delightful hideaway is a gilded dream of a place—as you would expect from interior designer Jacques Garcia. The hotel styles itself on a bygone era of travel, and every aspect of the design is one part sentimentality, one part sophisticate. (For example, upended vintage steamer trunks serve as bar fridges in the rooms, which are decorated with vintage maps, old prints, gilt frames and swathes of Parisian-style silk.) But it's The Atrium, The Parlour, the Library Bar and the Rooftop where the magic really beg Lush, elegant and completely beguil each of these dining spaces has beer created with attention to décor as w as cuisine. The mood may be French but the atmosphere is warm, chatty firmly American. All are wonderful spaces to meet with friends, or have romantic night. Book a room for ful effect. Baz Luhrmann and Catherine Martin often escape their Greenwich townhouse for a night here when the want some time away. *1170 Broadwa* *www.thenomadhotel.com*

Clockwise from top left: Joseph Leonard,
Freemans, bagels on Broadway and Café
Sabarsky in the Neue Galerie.
Opposite: Joseph Leonard.

GRAMERCY PARK HOTEL The Gramercy's rooftop terrace, which is called simply the Gramercy Terrace, is quite possibly one of the most coolly glamorous rooftop terraces in town. Designed so you can look out over much of the Gramercy Park neighbourhood, including the private Gramercy Park, this high-above-the-sky hangout is a symphony in green, black and white. The furniture is seriously gorgeous, there are different rooms for those who wish to have a function and the food is, well, just fab. *2 Lexington Avenue. www.gramercyparkhotel.com*

HARLOW Love the name. Love the restaurant even more. Like the Hollywood star who was famous for her long locks, seductive poses and sexy walk, Harlow is not shy when it comes to making an entrance. When it opened in 2013, New York's elite went into a tizz. *W* magazine commented: 'With its Dorothy Draper-esque decor, the venue fittingly evokes a sense of true Old Hollywood glamour …' It's still creating a buzz, and probably will be for some time. Find a classy date and then head for one of Harlow's corners for a truly sophisticated New York evening. *111 East 56th Street. www.harlownyc.com*

JEFFREY'S GROCERY A neighbourhood favourite, this place is often so busy you need to wait for a table. That's fairly common for places in New York, but this one is worth the patience. Its menu is 'highbrow hearty', which means it's good ol' fashioned American food done in a fancy West Village way. Think: eggs benedict with crispy pork-belly rillette. If you can't get a table, go for the bar: the action there is almost more entertaining, especially after midnight. Loud but loveable. A marvellous neighborhood diner, done the cheeky Manhattan way. *172 Waverly Place. www.jeffreysgrocery.com*

JOSEPH LEONARD This atmospheric little bolthole feels like your perfect drinking spot; you know, the one on the corner where everyone knows your name. Well, they should here because the interior is about as small as a drink coaster! With less than a dozen tables and a few barstools, it can feel 'intimate'— and the line to get in can sometimes be longer than the space itself—but the atmosphere inside is so inviting you won't mind sharing elbow space with strangers. The aesthetic is 'upmarket flea market' (old suitcases and vintage ladders), and the mood is classic tavern, with a great menu to match. Everything is incredibly cheap, too. (Lobster for $10?) *170 Waverly Place. www.josephleonard.com*

L'ABSINTHE It may be the bastion of the blue-blooded elite, but it's still one of the most beautiful bistros in Manhattan. With an interior that's a perfect replica of a classic, turn-of-the-century French bistro, L'Absinthe delivers as much in ambiance as it does in food and flavour. All the details, from the zinc bar and brass

The Lion restaurant in Greenwich Village: a favourite for many New Yorkers.

rails to the French menu, put patrons in the mood for the menu, which—although it's said to have gone down in quality— is adored by New York's Francophiles. *227 East 67th Street. www.labsinthe.com*

 THE LION Ah, The Lion. What can I say about my favourite dining place? To begin with, it features an interior that's completely unexpected. You walk into what looks like a very sophisticated bar, and then emerge into a double-height dining room that soars up, cathedral-like, to a stained-glass skylight. Around the room, covering the dark walls in a double-height gallery of prints, is an intriguingly eclectic collection of artworks, including photographs from the archives of *The Daily News*, and quirky prints, too. It's a beautiful space in which to have dinner, and chat, and laugh, and make memories, and consequently people linger until very late. It's that kind of place. *62 West 9th Street. www.thelionnyc.com*

THE PENINSULA If you've been to New York before but are travelling with someone who hasn't, and you want to show them some of the city's 'old glamour', then head to the rooftop terrace of The Peninsula Hotel for one of the best views of Fifth Avenue and the Manhattan skyline. Order a martini, watch the sunlight sink between the skyscrapers and envelop the city in pink, and toast the fact that you're in New York. Completely decadent. The place used to be a famous pick-up joint for well-heeled Manhattan execs, but thankfully it's now less of a desperate scene and attracts more of an after-work and late-night crowd. *700 Fifth Avenue. www.newyork.peninsula.com*

SCHILLER'S LIQUOR BAR
This is the kind of New York bar you expect (or hope) to find in New York: slightly retro, with loads of old-fashioned ambiance. It makes sense when you discover the man behind it is Keith McNally, who brought New York Balthazar, Odeon and Pastis. And, just as Pastis helped revive the Meatpacking District, Schiller's has regenerated the Lower East Side, a previously outlying neighbourhood, and turned it into a go-to zone for top fare. The beauty of Schiller's is that it looks like it's always been there. Mirrors are carefully made to look old, walls are tiled like subway stations, and the floor is black-and-white chequerboard. Even the curved bar is timber and zinc, with a perfect patina. It's been so well done that even the grumble-bums in the neighbourhood have grudgingly accepted it. *131 Rivington Street. www.schillersny.com*

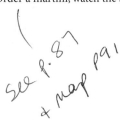
see p. 87
+ map p91

The bold, emerald-green, Irish-style Breslin bar in the Ace Hotel.
Opposite: The Gramercy Park Hotel's sunny rooftop terrace restaurant and
Bryant Park Grill.

A MEANDER
THROUGH
MANHATTAN'S
NEIGHBOURHOODS

NoHo, ProCro, SoBro, FiDi, NoLIta, BoHo, CanDo, ViVa … Once New Yorkers knew when a neighbourhood had become popular because its name was shortened to a catchy acronym, but now there's all kind of weirdly initialised words. I can't keep up! What the hell is a ViVa? Sounds like a washing-up liquid …
—An anonymous New Yorker overhead on the subway, discussing the Manhattan habit of abbreviating place names

New York is the biggest collection of villages in the world.
—Alistair Cooke

New York City isn't a city. Not really. It's an elegantly eclectic assortment of urban villages, all threaded onto avenues like a dazzling necklace around the neckline of Manhattan.

To make things more complicated, there are villages within villages, dubbed micro-villages. And then, inside these, even smaller ones: mini-villages.

Uptown, in the Upper West Side, for example, there's a hidden quarter near West 95th Street called Pomander Walk, which is so different from the rest of New York that it looks like it's been lifted from a movie-set of an English hamlet in England—leading some locals to dub it 'the Downtown (Abbey) of uptown'.

To make things even more interesting (and perhaps confusing), each of these villages—the sprawling villages, the micro-villages, the mini-villages, even the secret villages—is starkly different from its neighbours. And sometimes the change can come as suddenly as stepping down off one kerb, walking across a street and stepping up onto another. I used to get nervous about the way Manhattan changed neighbourhoods so quickly (it scared me to think you could walk from a glamorous area to a grungier one within a block), but now I've come to love the way New York surprises you with its village variations. Every corner brings a new surprise; every turn a new street scene. That's the beauty of New York's neighbour hoods: they're as disparate as its architecture, its food, its passions and its people.

This book is predominantly about style and design destinations in Manhattan, and the easiest way to categorise it is by these villages—and by taking you on a wander through them. This is how I've come to know New York: by exploring it gently, wandering from one urban village to the other in a desultory, meandering, joyously indulgent fashion. And so here, in no particular order, is my guide to what I think are New York City's most interesting villages—and some of the fabulous stores, sights, hotels, gardens, architecture, and other intriguing and whimsical things hidden within them. It's by no means comprehensive, but it will give you a taste of the New York that I love. I hope it inspires you to explore more of this marvellous old town.

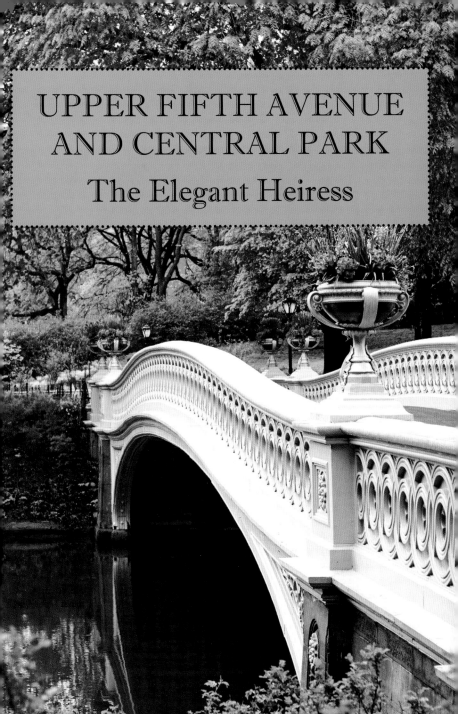

UPPER FIFTH AVENUE AND CENTRAL PARK

The Elegant Heiress

Upper Fifth Ave & Central Park

Fifth Avenue is the Jacqueline Kennedy Onassis of avenues: always immaculate and always discreet, and therefore unsure of why it still finds itself in the glare of the media spotlight. (Jackie herself had an apartment at 1040 Fifth in her final years: it was a fitting pairing.) Not many avenues have this problem. Most of the world's glamour avenues, such as Boulevard Saint-Germain and those in Beverly Hills, rather like being the centre of attention. Not Fifth. Certainly not the section that runs parallel to Central Park, anyway. It would prefer complete anonymity.

This is the part of New York where discretion is not just advised but followed in an almost religious fashion. Residents here don't parade themselves around. They walk, as Diana Vreeland advised, with a 'very quiet step' and live their lives in a similar fashion. And while

they dress in designer labels—Oscar de la Renta, Hubert de Givenchy, Christian Dior—they've usually had those coats and frocks for years.

It's because of this reluctance to 'show off' that this part of Fifth Avenue isn't prone to publicising its best bits. Everything here is as neatly tucked away as the corners of the 1000-thread-count sheets on the Duxiana beds. It does have its high-profile icons—the Met, the Guggenheim, The Plaza, The Frick—but the really good bits are often hidden out of sight.

So here's a list to launch your New York adventure in style. I think this enclave is perhaps one of the most delightful corners in Manhattan, if not the most impressive. (You'll be suffering neck ache from all the craning you'll be doing to look up at the buildings.) Welcome to where the

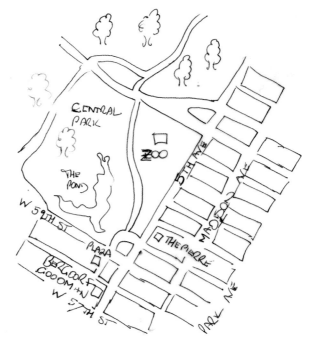

truly privileged live, shop, drink and generally live the grand Manhattan life.

STAY: If you want to fork out for a memorable night, **The F. Scott Fitzgerald Suite at The Plaza** is the place to do it. Designed by Oscar-winning costume designer and Baz Luhrmann's other half, Catherine Martin, the dramatic Art Deco space was inspired by Scott and Zelda, both devoted patrons of The Plaza. The suite features photos of the duo, Scott's complete works, documentaries and movies, and beautiful coffee-table books that evoke languorous summers on Long Island and New York in the roaring twenties. *768 Fifth Avenue. www.plazany.com*

DRINK: The Salon de Ning rooftop bar at The Peninsula hotel was designed to evoke the glamour of 1930s Shanghai, although you just have to look outside to know you're in Manhattan! It has one of the best views of Upper Fifth Avenue in the city, and makes for an amazing evening if you get there before sunset. *700 Fifth Avenue. www.newyork.peninsula.com*

WANDER: Philanthropist Nell Singer funded the creation of **The Lilac Walk in Central Park**, a small path at the northern border of the Sheep Meadow, and what a gloriously scented idea it was. One of the most beautiful walks in Central Park, the Lilac Walk is planted with twenty-three varieties of this beautiful flower, including the spectacular Japanese tree lilac (*Syringa reticulata*). Inhale the fragrance and marvel at one of nature's loveliest creations. (Best seen in late spring and summer.) *Between Central Park West and Fifth Avenue, Central Park. www.centralpark.com*

VISIT: A must-see for lovers of design and art, **The Frick Collection** is often described as the smallest, densest and finest collection of art in New York. It's an exquisite, once-private 1914 mansion full of sumptuous rooms, period furniture and artistic masterpieces. My favourite part is the serene interior Garden Court, a grand, Roman-style atrium with vaulted ceilings and exotic palms. The Russell Page-designed outdoor garden on 70th Street is also a horticultural poem of sheer loveliness, with just the right amounts of simplicity and detail, lawn and leaf, and classical and modern. It was designed to be viewed from the street or through the arched windows of the Reception Hall like an Impressionist painting. An interesting idea, but it works. *1 East 70th Street. www.frick.org*

EXPLORE: 'A park within a park', **The Conservatory Garden** is one of the best-kept secrets of Central Park. The entrance is via the ornate Vanderbilt Gate, which was formerly part of the Vanderbilt mansion, and it can be tricky to find, which makes it all the more like a secret garden. (Fittingly, there is a statue of *The Secret Garden*'s author Frances Hodgson Burnett inside.) This is the only formal garden in Central Park and is composed around English, French and Italian planting schemes and designs. The Italian garden features the renowned crab-apple walk (an amazing sight in spring) and a wonderful wisteria pergola, while the French garden offers spring tulips, and the English garden magnolias and lilacs. (There is a bloom schedule on the park's website.) The garden is best seen in early spring (April, May), when the famed cherry blossoms are out. Truly one of the city's most beautiful corners.
Fifth Avenue and 105th Street.
www.centralpark.com

*I just want to go through Central Park and watch folks passing by.
Spend the whole day watching people. I miss that.*
—Barack Obama

SPOT: A signature feature of the Fifth Avenue skyline, the rooftop of **The Pierre**'s ornate shape (above) is an architectural treasure. It was once the most glamorous ballroom in Manhattan—and a place for high society to escape Depression-era New York. The ballroom was shuttered in the early 1970s and forgotten about for nearly twenty years. Lost to time, it was regarded by Pierre staff of as a kind of 'grand attic' to shove unwanted furniture. It was finally sold in 1988 to Australian heiress Lady Mary Fairfax, who converted it into one of the most opulent private residences in the city. (It included a 3500-square-foot ballroom, a Belgian marble double staircase, a 20-foot-high Palladian windows, a curved 23-foot ceiling and huge terraces overlooking Central Park.) It was later re-listed for US$70 million; at that time the highest price ever for a New York residence. It was such a symbol of wealth that the makers of the film *Meet Joe Black* cast the penthouse as the residence of Anthony Hopkins' character. To locate it, look for the French-style Mansard roof on Fifth Avenue. *2 East 61st Street.*

see Paley Park p96

FASHION, STYLE
AND DESIGN DESTINATIONS

You see? I told you! This is how the grown-ups dress.
—one 12-year-old girl to another, overheard on the Upper East Side

ASSOULINE Assouline's first US bookstore is an elegant little boutique tucked away in The Plaza Hotel. Now, if you haven't been to The Plaza for a stickybeak, here's a good excuse to go. The hotel's interior is deservedly famous, but Assouline's bookstore inside is just as gorgeous. To find it, walk into the grand gilded foyer, turn left (ignore the 'Guests Only' sign), and then head up the ornate gold stairs to the mezzanine. (There's also a glam bar on the way up, to the left.) The store is tiny but it's filled with Assouline's signature glossy coffee-table titles on fashion, photography, travel and society. It also carries beautiful vintage books (and not just the Assouline imprint), plus unusual book-themed ideas and gifts for the fussy bibliophile. (Candles that smell like books, for example.) I once found an old Jackie O book, signed by Jackie herself. One day I'll buy a few Slim Aaron photographs from here. *The Plaza Hotel, mezzanine level, 768 Fifth Avenue. www.assouline.com*

BETHESDA TERRACE AND ARCADE, CENTRAL PARK Most people love Central Park because it offers a much-needed respite from the havoc and traffic of Manhattan. But if you're a design and architecture fan, there's a special place that will appeal. The Bethesda Arcade is a 5292-square-foot, 16-foot-high columned chamber and a walkway covered with exquisite tiles that is, quite literally, a work of art. It's arguably the architectural centrepiece of the 843-acre Central Park. Built in the mid 1860s, the 15 876 elaborately patterned tiles were designed by Jacob Wrey Mould, who used tiles manufactured by the Minton Company of Stoke-on-Trent, England. By 2000, the ceiling was badly in need of some TLC (tile love 'n care). In 2005, thanks to a US$7 million makeover and a dedicated team of conservationists, restoration work began. It took four months to number and document the tiles, and then about 24 000 hours to repair the tiles, which cost $200 to $300 apiece to produce. It's an incredible chamber that leads to another superb sight, the magnificent Bethesda Fountain, and beyond is one of the loveliest watery vistas in the park, looking over the

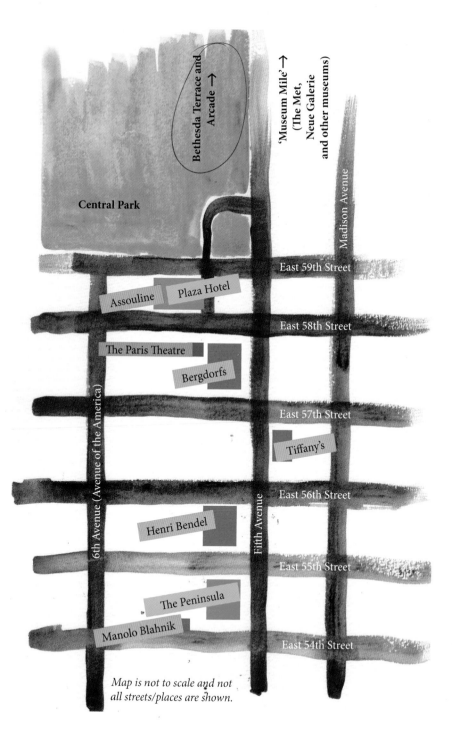

'Museum Mile' →
(The Met,
Neue Galerie
and other museums)

Bethesda Terrace and
Arcade →

Central Park

Madison Avenue

East 59th Street

Assouline   Plaza Hotel

East 58th Street

The Paris Theatre

Bergdorfs

6th Avenue (Avenue of the America)

East 57th Street

Tiffany's

East 56th Street

Henri Bendel

Fifth Avenue

East 55th Street

The Peninsula

Manolo Blahnik

East 54th Street

*Map is not to scale and not
all streets/places are shown.*

boats of Loeb Boathouse. The fountain features an 8-foot bronze statue of a female winged angel, and beneath her, four 4-foot cherubs representing Temperance, Purity, Health and Peace. Bethesda Terrace is now one of the most popular spots in Central Park, and justly so: it's a haven of serenity and greenery. *Just inside Central Park, enter from Fifth Avenue and East 72nd Street.* www.centralparknyc.org

BLOOMINGDALE'S Bloomie's regular shoes sales are famous (and the Boxing Day sales are madness). Finding a pair left in your size is another matter. Never mind. The thrill is in the rush of it all, as buyers scrabble to grab the heels that catch their eye. If you don't have the mental (or leg) strength to handle sale action, go in non-sale time and allow yourself an indulgence. This place always offers something lovely. *1000 3rd Avenue. www.bloomingdales.com*

The Bethesda Terrace and a mannequin on Madison Avenue. Opposite: Henri Bendel.

HENRI BENDEL Okay, so it's far from being a secret among locals, but it deserves a mention because not enough tourists know about this shopping gem. Most people do Saks, Barneys and Bergdorf Goodman, but Henri Bendel is far more intimate and exquisite, and the window displays are always sublime. The petite interior is like a doll's house, the shopping is fabulous (look for the store's signature chocolate-and-white striped gifts to the left of the entrance; fashion journos flying into New York love buying these for friends at home), and the atmosphere is always lively and fun. But the best part is the rear area on the second floor, which is so hidden away that many Bendel shoppers miss it in the swing from floor to floor. This is where some of the best gifts, books, handbags, scarves and other gorgeous goods in New York can be found. The books here are always well curated, and the handbags and scarves ... well, let's just say you might be here a while! Expensive, but exquisite. *712 Fifth Avenue. www.henribendel.com*

NEUE GALERIE Not only does the Neue have a great art and design bookshop, and an extraordinarily beautiful interior (don't miss the ornate staircase), but the exhibits are always worthwhile, even the ones that seem abbreviated. (I once saw a Klimt exhibition here: there were only a handful of paintings but it was surprisingly memorable.) And don't miss coffee at the sublime Café Sabarsky overlooking the park; it's modelled after a nineteenth-century Viennese coffee house and is one of the prettiest places for afternoon tea on the Upper East Side. All in all, the Neue is a real gem. *1048 Fifth Avenue. www.neuegalerie.org*

MANOLO BLAHNIK Manolo's store is so discreet that it's difficult to find, but it's always buzzing with shoe buyers. For a while this was the preferred New York shoe for fashion people, and although many have diversified their tastes, Manolo still pulls them in. (You should see the commotion and hysteria when the store has its sales.) The shoes are not cheap, but they're beautiful—and classic. No wonder they're considered collector's items. *31 West 54th Street. manoloblahnik.com*

METROPOLITAN MUSEUM OF ART AND THE IRIS AND B. GERALD CANTOR ROOF GARDEN Most people head to the sky to get the best views of Manhattan—either by using a helicopter, joining the queue for the Empire State Building or (one of my favourites) taking the lifts to the top of the Rockefeller Centre (it has superb for views of the Empire State, midtown and downtown).

However, there are other ways to get up and above the city, and one of them is the Iris and B. Gerald Cantor Roof Garden of the Met. It's one of those places many of us never think to go when we're wandering up and down Museum Mile, but it's definitely worth the effort. Spend a few hours exploring the amazing American Wing of the museum, and then head up to the roof in the golden light of the late afternoon to see the city dazzle. There's a cute café and bar, which come alive on warm nights, especially on Friday and Saturday evenings when lots of locals head there. Oh, and while you're at the Met, don't miss visiting the bookstore. It offers an astounding book selection, as well as reproductions of statuettes and other objects, and a dazzling jewellery selection with Byzantine- and Egyptian-inspired baubles. *1000 Fifth Avenue. www.metmuseum.org*

PALEY PARK New York doesn't have as many gardens as Paris or London, so when you stumble across them, usually by happy accident as you're marching from one place to another, it's a wonderful surprise. Paley Park is one of these places. This 'pocket park' is situated on West 53rd between Fifth and Madison, and has been variously described 'a corner of quiet delights' and 'an urban oasis'. There are ivy-covered walls, a grand waterfall, an ornate gate and an overhead canopy formed from locust trees. There's even a piece of the Berlin Wall— complete with bullet holes. It's a much-welcomed respite after hours striding up and down Fifth Avenue. *West 53rd Street, between Fifth Avenue and Madison Avenue.*

TIFFANY & CO. Ah, Tiffany's. What other jewellery could incite such a sigh? Okay, so reportedly Cartier does better diamond rings but Tiffany's has the marketing down pat. In fact, the pale robin's-egg blue colour has been copyrighted by the company. That particular hue was originally chosen because it was Empress Eugenie's favourite shade, and she was at that time a fashion plate imitated the world over. Turquoise gems were also popular in the nineteenth century. Tiffany sparkles have appeared in no less than forty-eight Hollywood films, the latest being Baz Luhrmann's *The Great Gatsby* (2013). But it was perhaps Audrey Hepburn, who really immortalised the store in *Breakfast at Tiffany's*. The store is worth a peek, just to say you've been there. And yes, the boxes are pretty, too. *727 Fifth Avenue. www.tiffany.com*

The Neue Galerie

SHOP: Bergdorf Goodman is set on the site of the former Vanderbilt mansion. This spectacularly ornate Beaux Arts-style store is the department store for ladies who lunch. (And businesswomen who don't, but still need outfits in a hurry.) There are eight floors of designer goodies but it feels like more, and you can become fatigued after a few loops. Everything here is luxury and then some—even the plush dressing rooms on floors two, three and four have swoon-worthy views of Central Park. Some BG devotees argue that the best part is the shoe department: divided into two floors, it has both mid-priced lines from the likes of Marc Jacobs and instantly covetable higher-end numbers from Manolo and co. If that isn't appealing enough for shoe lov-ers, there is now—wait for it—an in-house Manolo Blahnik Custom BB Boutique, where you can order your own customised Manolo Blahnik heels. (Shipping from the Italian factory takes six weeks, but you can choose and order online, so they're waiting when you arrive in New York.) My favourite customised Manolos are the leopard pumps, inspired by Brigitte Bardot, but there is a selection of heel heights and fabric styles to choose from. Another great place inside the store is the restaurant at the top, which features an interior by Kelly Wearstler and views over Fifth Avenue and Central Park. (Note: If you want to learn more about BG, try to source the great film *Scatter My Ashes at Bergdorf's*.) *754 Fifth Avenue. www.bergdorfgoodman.com*

The Carlyle Hotel.
Opposite: A window display
of real and faux luggage on
Upper Fifth Avenue.

BOOK: An Architecture Tour of The Plaza. The private tours of The Plaza Hotel's sumptuous rooms are led by architectural historian and author Francis Morrone, who narrates New York's glamorous past with raconteurish wit. Included are anecdotes about Truman Capote's notorious Party of the Century at The Plaza, also known as The Black and White Ball, which was held in 'the most beautiful room in New York' (according to Capote). It was so famous that a book was written about it. Tours are normally for 20 people but you might be able to swing a private one for a small group. *768 Fifth Avenue. www.theplazany.com/history/architectural-society-tour*

Dior

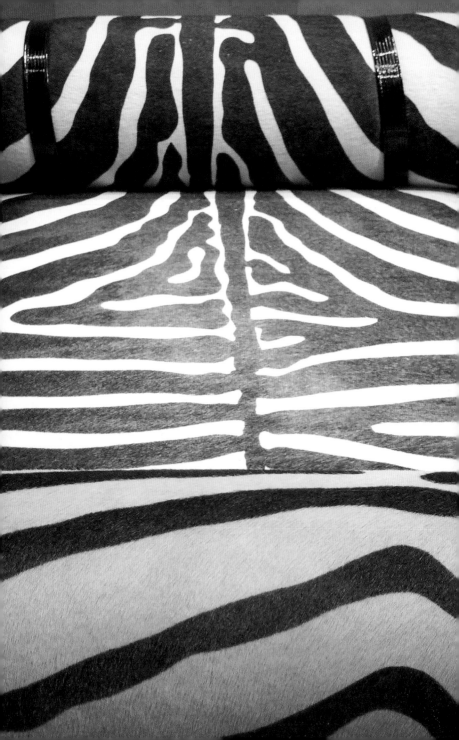

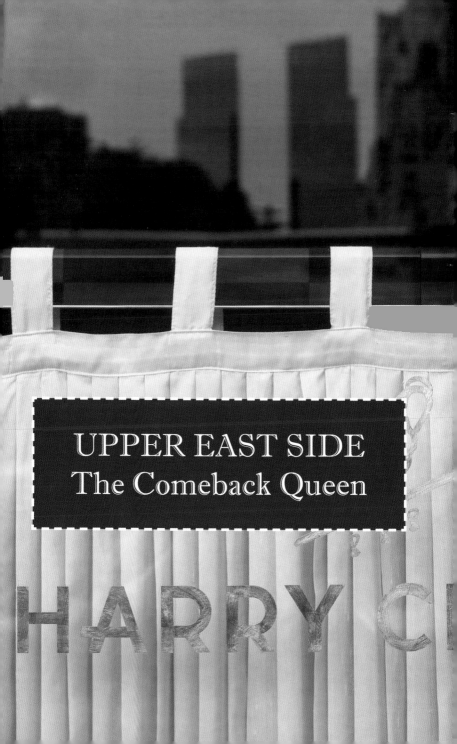

Upper East Side

You can never be too rich or too thin, or own too much blue and white porcelain.
—Babe Paley (who could have been talking about Upper East Siders)

The Upper East Side (UES) reminds me of Ms Elizabeth Taylor. When questioned about her acting ability, Ms Taylor once retorted: 'I don't have to act; I'm a star', and you can almost hear the UES saying the same thing. It's New York's version of a grand, still-glamorous screen legend who has seen it all and is still standing tall (and looking pretty darn fabulous, darling). It's never worried about whether it's 'in' or 'out', or 'hot' or 'not'. It also doesn't care that for the last few years some people have considered it uncool to live uptown. It is what it is and it makes no excuses for it. And for that you have to admire it.

Of course, the Upper East Side has the pedigree—and the wealth—to pull off such a personality. The scent of old money hangs in the air here like a cloud of Guerlain. The streets are punctuated by Chloé-clad women sporting jewels that could rival the masterpieces in the Met's Costume Institute (those Sotheby's estate sales are marvellous), while the residences are the kind you see in *Architectural Digest* magazine. This is the home of Holly Golightlys in their little black Givenchys and va-va-voom pearls. It's the land of the chauffeur-driven town car and the brass-buttoned doorman (both of whom make getting around on heels much easier), and of the personal dog walker and the white-gloved maître d' who knows your name. It's the kind of neighbourhood where you are expected to know your Sèvres dinner services and your Vigée Le Bruns tables. This is true Jay Gatz territory: both he and his creator F. Scott Fitzgerald felt at home here, amid the gilded ceilings, cavernous dressing rooms and triplex-with-terrace penthouses.

In saying all this, there is something unerringly pleasant about walking around the Upper East Side. It's polished, tasteful, measured and well-mannered, and its neat streetscapes and boutiques are surprisingly calming. (The only time I've ever heard a siren here is when President Obama's cavalcade drove past.) Most of the woman are so well put together that—as in Paris—it's a lesson in style just to walk around.

THE REVIVAL OF THE UPPER EAST SIDE (UES)

The Upper East Side has gone through more ups and downs than Liza Minnelli and—like Miss Minnelli—has recently emerged looking better than ever. Gone is the palour of the 2K era, when it lost the sparkle and sheen, and in its place is a shimmering, shimmying (think of Liza singing Beyoncé in *Sex and the City 2*), and altogether sexier new UES. In the past few years, more than fifty stores have opened, mostly north of Barneys, among them Céline, Bottega Veneta, Pucci, Proenza Schouler, Alice and Olivia, Anya Hindmarch, and Kate Spade. Meanwhile, long-time UES retailers, such as Oscar de la Renta, Lanvin and Chanel, are expanding to try and keep up.

The demographic has also changed. Once UES fashion was firmly tailored to high society socialites. Now there's a haute-meets-hybrid mix of high-end and high-street designs; just as the fashion editors advocate. Yes, the UES habituée has become happily multifarious. Take a walk along Madison Avenue from 60th to 70th Street today and you'll encounter a harmonious mix of well-heeled locals and ballet-flat toting tourists and students, poor young wannabes, and affluent, gently aging grand dames. Few would have thought it a decade or two ago, but the UES has become one of the most diversified, dilettantish shopping precincts north of the Flatiron.

You've also got all the architectural eye candy to ogle, plus the city's greatest museums, and of course more stylish stores than you can throw a camel Birkin at … No wonder it's still the preferred haunt of a certain well-heeled demographic.

To make things more interesting, the UES has recently undergone something of an urban facelift, and has emerged a fresher version of its former self. Gone is the slightly weary, slightly dreary neighbourhood that faded when the glamour set decided to move downtown, and in its place is a shiny, sleek new UES—just as it used to be in its heyday. Once Ralph Lauren did a fixer-upper job on the grand, gracious, former Vanderbilt-owned mansion at 888 Madison Avenue, opposite his already-famous Rhinelander Mansion store; others soon followed. Now the old neighbourhood is sparkling with style and life again.

Oh, yes, the Upper East Side is well and truly on the comeback trail.

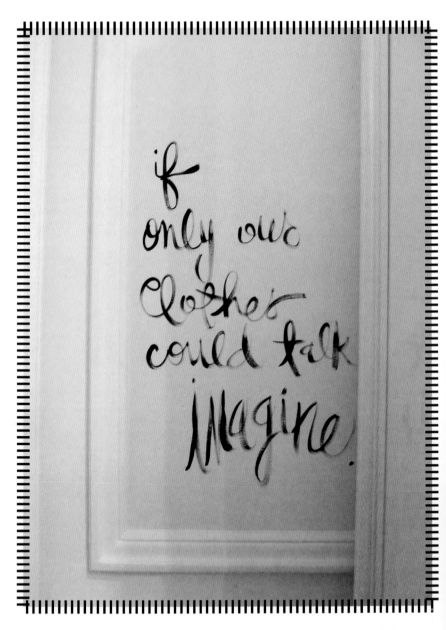

Wall 'art' at Lilly Pulitzer.

Kate Spade and Hermès.
Opposite: Architecture on the UES.

• •

Uptown is the new Downtown.
—A poster in Kate Spade's new flagship store on Madison Avenue

STAY: The Surrey (Chanel-esque colour palettes and subdued luxury) or **The Mark** (striped, monochromatic glamour from design genius Jacques Grange). *The Surrey: 20 East 76th Street. www.thesurrey.com; The Mark: 25 East 77th Street. www.themarkhotel.com*

DRINK: The Surrey's black-and-beige, faux-quilted, Coco Chanel-inspired bar or **Bemelmans Bar** at **The Carlyle**, a true New York classic with grace and charm. And if you can catch Woody Allen playing with his band at The Carlyle it's even better. *The Surrey: 20 East 76th Street. www.thesurrey. com The Carlyle: 35 East 76th Street. www. rosewoodhotels.com/en/the-carlyle-new-york*

WANDER: Henderson Place is a pretty, well-preserved enclave of Victorian-era New York presented in a teeny cul-de-sac. Great for architecture lovers. *Off 86th Street, near East End Avenue.*

BE INSPIRED: If you love design and style, you can't miss either the handsome Rhinelander Mansion or the former Vanderbilt Mansion directly opposite, both now homes for **Ralph Lauren's** elegant collections. Go for the architecture, the interiors, the merchandising or the famously grand staircase. Or just go for the clothes. *867 Madison Avenue. www.ralphlauren.com*

ARCHITECTURAL TRAIL

The quarter between 70th Street and 72nd Street, and 3rd Avenue and Fifth Avenue is home to all kinds of astonishing architecture, ranging from grand mansions to mini chateaux. If you love looking at houses, a wander around here will reward with opulent Beaux Arts and Gilded Age glories.

Start at the legendary setting for Holly Golightly's apartment in *Breakfast at Tiffany's:* 169 East 71st Street. Then meander up and down 70th, 71st and 72nd streets, and eventually make your way to Bunny Mellon's fourteen-room former townhouse at 125 East 70th Street (above, far right). Built in 1965 by the banking-heir husband of the

famously stylish horticulturist (who wore Balenciaga when gardening—how glamorous), it may look bijoux from the outside, but it opens up to a spectacularly beautiful mansion, which was recently up for sale for almost US$50 million.

And if you loved Carrie's building in *Sex and the City,* then you're in the right neighbourhood: beautiful old buildings are in glorious abundance. The irony is, while Carrie's fictional apartment building was supposedly located at 245 East 73rd Street (it's not really there), the 'real' apartment building shot for the series and film is further downtown at 66 Perry Street in the West Village.

SHOP: Decoration and Design Building (DDB) If you're an interior designer, a decorator or just someone who just lives fabrics, furnishings, furniture and homewares, you are going to go wild here. This is the place many New York interior designers start when they want to source fabrics for clients, because almost every major design house is here, under one roof. Not all of them, of course, but a significant number, including Alexa Hampton, Armani, Barbara Barry, B&B Italia, Baker Lifestyles, Brunschwig & Fils, Christian Lacroix, Christopher Farr, Clarence House … you get the picture. (These are just some of the As, Bs and Cs: I haven't even reached the rest of the alphabet.) It bills itself as the Western Hemisphere's premier design centre, and it wouldn't be far off the mark. The 120 showrooms represent more than 3000 design names, and products include fabric, wall coverings, furniture, carpets, lighting, antiques and accessories. Every time I come I see something I covet. Last time it was a hot-pink zebra print chaise longue. So New York! It can be overwhelming, so work out which showrooms you want to visit and consult the index at the entrance to the building. If you get stuck, the concierge can help. Tip: leave an entire morning or afternoon for here, you'll need it. *979 3rd Avenue. www.ddbuilding.com*

Ralph Lauren.
Opposite, a window display
at Bergdorf Goodman.

FASHION, STYLE
AND DESIGN DESTINATIONS

ALEXIS BITTAR The first sign that you're entering a store with a striking difference is the life-sized zebra that welcomes shoppers. It's a symbol of Alexis Bittar's bold take on life, and on jewellery. Best known for his Lucite bangles and block rings, Bittar has expanded his collection to include precious metals and semiprecious stones. Wild indeed. *1100 Madison Avenue. www.alexisbittar.com*

ARGOSY BOOK STORE Argosy offers some of the best vintage books in the city, stocked in a dignified old bookstore that looks like a rich uncle's library, complete with Kelly green walls and a charming mezzanine. *116 East 59th Street. www.argosybooks.com*

ANYA HINDMARCH The British handbag designer has just opened her new New York store, and it's as stylish as her designs, with smart mahogany chests and armoires full of leather loveliness. There's also a bespoke tailor in-store, to help you design your perfect weekender. And the bag, too. *795 Madison Avenue. www.anyahindmarch.com*

BOND NO. 9 The beauty of Bond No. 9's collection of city-centric scents is that they reflect the neighbourhoods they're named after. I love the High Line fragrance; just as refreshing as the actual place. There are also other New York-centric fragrances available, all of them lovelier than the city itself. *897 Madison Ave. www.bondno9.com*

BUCK HOUSE Like its name, Buck House is an unusual emporium of antiques, art and jewellery. The store is named after its owner, Deborah Buck, an artist, author, entrepreneur and tastemaker, and features not only her own art and signature line of fabric, wallpaper and furniture, but also wonderfully eclectic pieces by others. She travels the world to curate her collection, and has been celebrated by the likes of *New York Times, Elle Decor, Architectural Digest, O Magazine* and *Metropolitan Home*. Her windows are particularly admired: the merchandising often portrays strong female personalities and their personal spaces, and come to life through the carefully created objects and backdrops. *1318 Madison Avenue. www.buckhouse.com*

CREEL AND GOW Creel and Gow is like the Manhattan version of Deyrolle in Paris—only with a distinctly New York look. And fewer lions, tigers, giraffes, chimpanzees. The fabulous collection of natural-history whimsy includes taxidermied specimens and artisanal objects. A true wunderkammern. The prettiest pieces are the peacocks. *131 East 70th Street. www.creelandgow.com*

EXTRAORDINARY In opening this store, the goal of Extraordinary's owner was stocking pieces 'you can't find on Google'. It's certainly a godsend for those bored by the selection of decorations at large department stores and online shopping sites. There are hand-painted mirrors, stunning vases in different shapes and colours, animal-shaped paperweights, small carousels and music boxes, and greeting cards that are so lovely, you'll want to buy a dozen to have at hand when you need them. *247 East 57th Street. www.extraordinaryny.com*

FIVESTORY The founder of Fivestory, Claire Distenfeld, used to work in art, but soon realised that shopping was her true love. This boutique is a tribute to her fine taste—and her experience as a die-hard shopper! When conceiving the store, she drew upon words like 'connoisseurship', 'curated', 'au courant' and 'luxury', and the store certainly reflects these values and ideas. It's a mix of uptown and downtown looks, from pretty frocks to the famous clutches by designer Olympia Le-Tan, which are made to look like books (think *La Femme Amoureuse* and *The Catcher in the Rye*). *18 East 69th Street. www.fivestoryny.com*

FRENCH SOLE AND FRENCH SOLE OUTLET STORE When it comes to dainty ballet flats, few do it better than French Sole. New Yorker and London lovelies have been donning this brand to get around town for years. You can never have too many ballet flats, and French Sole sells hundreds of colours. This boutique is the brand's 23-year-old flagship store and sells all the covetable shades, but if you don't fancy forking out $150–200 there's also an outlet store, conveniently located across the street. (Look for the sale bins where you can score a pair for just $59.) *985 and 976 Lexington Avenue. www.frenchsoleshoes.com*

Argosy Book Store

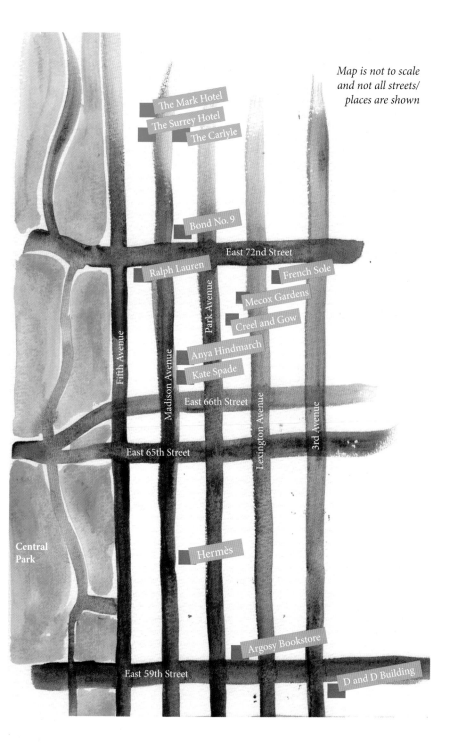

Map is not to scale and not all streets/ places are shown

The Mark Hotel

The Surrey Hotel

The Carlyle

Bond No. 9

East 72nd Street

Ralph Lauren

French Sole

Mecox Gardens

Creel and Gow

Anya Hindmarch

Kate Spade

Park Avenue

Fifth Avenue

Madison Avenue

East 66th Street

Lexington Avenue

3rd Avenue

East 65th Street

Central Park

Hermès

Argosy Bookstore

East 59th Street

D and D Building

SHOP: Ralph Lauren is synonymous with the Upper East Side. When he renovated the former Rhinelander mansion at 867 Madison Avenue in 1986 and made it his flagship store, it not only changed the retail landscape of the UES completely but also the shopping experience. Wandering through the store was like wandering through a Nancy Meyers-style film set of a wealthy person's abode, complete with books, galleries of black-and-white portraits and other personal touches. Then when Ralph Lauren commissioned a similar limestone Beaux Arts mansion directly opposite it in 2010, it, too, regenerated the area. The designer also has two other stores nearby, including a children's boutique, but it's these two gracious architectural beauties that really make people go 'wow'. Even if you can't afford to buy Ralph Lauren's clothes, simply wander around inside for the interior design, the fit-out, the merchandising and the whole grand show. *888 Madison Avenue. www.ralphlauren.com*

SHOP: Kate Spade's newest store on the Upper East Side is also now its flagship boutique, and rightly so. The sweet, townhouse-style store is a multi-level, candy-and-cocktail coloured dream of a retail space, with covetable things arranged in every corner, from vintage books to fuschia sun dresses and fabulous handbags. (Gorgeous heels, too.) *789 Madison Avenue. www.katespade.com*

GRACIOUS HOME As the name implies, Gracious Home is a lovely place, full of lovely pieces. But it's more than a store full of sophisticated dinnerware and table linens. Staff will assist if you're looking for something special, or you have a difficult piece that needs work. A friend of mine took a piece of furniture there that wasn't put together well, and they happily fixed it for her. (They also have more stores in Chelsea and in Upper West Side.) *1220 3rd Avenue. www.gracioushome.com*

HERMÈS Most of the style set is already familiar with the French house of Hermès. However, this store is still worth a visit, and not just for the always-amazing window displays. (When I was there recently, the mannequins were 'framed' by piles of books.) Their accessories are some of the most coveted in the world, and it's not surprising; even the blankets are beautiful. But it's the fragrances that are really lovely, including the recently released Un Jardin Sur Le Toit (A Garden on the Roof). If you can't stretch the funds to a handbag, treat yourself to one of the pretty bracelets. *691 Madison Avenue. www.hermes.com*

JULIUS LOWY FRAME & RESTORING CO. It was the architect Stanford White who first began to design custom picture frames for his friends, because he felt that a frame could be as important as the artwork it held. A century on, art lovers are still seeking that perfect, unique frame to showcase their prints and paintings, and Julius Lowy is the store they go to. Founded in 1907, this Manhattan framing and art conservation company has established a reputation for fine frames. It's the kind of place where you'll discover frames that aren't anywhere else in the world—it is a mecca for people who collect art. Their store is so well known that they curated an exhibition, 'A Change of Taste: From the Gilded Age to the Craftsman Aesthetic', which was featured in *Elle Decor* and other media. Fine lines, indeed. *223 East 80th Street. www.lowy1907.com*

LILLY PULITZER Surprising and delightful—and that's just the interior design, with its pink walls, and witty writing and prints. The collections are feminine and flirty without being too girlie: think Babe Paley in Palm Beach in the 1960s. *1020 Madison Avenue. www.lillypulitzer.com*

LISA PERRY Lisa Perry's boutique is a fun stop for shoppers in search of bright, bold, eye-catching clothes and quirky housewares. Known for her 21st-century take on mid-century style, the designer's line of apparel, accessories and housewares offers popping primary colours and geometric shapes. *988 Madison Avenue. www.lisaperrystyle.com*

MON AMOUR PARIS ACCESSORIES The name may be cute-ish, but the collections are pure class. This French-themed boutique is a real shopping gem, offering splendid costume jewellery that looks more expensive than it actually is. The Parisian expat owners buy mostly from small-scale, local designers who create unique and budget-friendly baubles that are brightly displayed on elegant white shelves. It also carries high-fashion coffee-table books, including three-book sets detailing the history of Chanel and Condé Nast *Traveller's Room with a View*. Jewellery fans adore it. It's particularly great for special one-of-a-kind, ready-to-wear pieces. *551 3rd Avenue.*

MECOX GARDENS Gardeners love Mecox Gardens. But you don't have to own a patch of greenery to come here. Even those with an apartment the size of a Post-It note will find something pretty. The original Mecox is in the Hamptons, where the still-existing store has become a garden empire. This outpost (citypost?) isn't as big but it's still stocked with gorgeous goods. Pieces range from artichoke-motif trays to canopy beds and armoires, and of course, gardening gorgeousness. A little piece of the Hamptons on the Upper East Side. *962 Lexington Avenue. www.mecox.com*

PROENZA SCHOULER One example of how Madison Avenue is morphing to accommodate a whole new UES demographic is the arrival of edgy designers such as Proenza Schouler. Once upon an UES day, nobody would have dreamed that a store such as this would sit happily near preppy haunts like Ralph Lauren, but now they do and—like the rich girl and the cool newcomer to school—they seem to get along beautifully. *822 Madison Avenue. www.proenzaschouler.com*

ROBERTA ROLLER RABBIT Those heading out of town to the South of France, St Barts or Harbour Island head here first, to stock up on brightly coloured resort wear and beautiful beach bags. Roberta Freymann scours the globe for amazing handworked textiles and accessories, but she also designs her own colour-block tunics and beach bags, which perfectly suit beach life. As well, she stocks sublime daybeds and end tables, if you want some of that St Barts chic in your own home. If you love the Calypso St Barth label, you'll probably like it here. (Note: I've heard customer service can be terrible, but I've had good experiences.) *1019 Lexington Avenue. www.robertarollerrabbit.com*

TENDER BUTTONS Who would have thought a button store could be so fascinating? This boutique stocks all kinds of buttons in every style, from silver, crystal, leather and wood, to faux ivory. There are also displays of rare buttons on the wall, just to add to the museum feel. Owner Millicent Safro is something of a button connoisseur and has attracted clients like Calvin Klein, Julia Roberts and Greta Garbo (perhaps she liked sewing too?). Great for those who sew and want an haute couture touch to their clothes. The most beautiful buttons are the coconut shell numbers. *143 East 62nd Street. www.tenderbuttons-nyc.com*

TINSEL TRADING COMPANY Such a lovely name, and such a lovely store! One friend calls this place 'haberdashery heaven', and it is certainly an eyeful of delights. The shelves are full of all kinds of pretty passementerie, from tassels to ribbons, buttons, fringes, feathers and floral garlands, and other decorative bits and bobs. I once saw a basket full of vintage wooden spools, which would have made for a gorgeous display. *828 Lexington Avenue. www.tinseltrading.com*

URSUS BOOKS AND PRINTS Like Argosy Book Store, Ursus is another great literary hideaway. Just ask the book-loving former presidents who have been spotted here, with their heads between the pages. There's a great selection of art books, plus rare titles and first editions in a range of subjects. *699 Madison Avenue. www.ursusbooks.com*

UPPER WEST SIDE
The Understated Intellectual

Nelson Fox: *Keep those West-Side liberal nuts, pseudo-intellectuals …*
Joe Fox: *Readers, Dad. They're called readers.*
Nelson Fox: *Don't do that, son. Don't romanticize them.*
—You've Got Mail

While the Upper East Side is gilded grandeur and upscale glamour, the Upper West Side (UWS) is upscale understated. It's not the UWS thing to display your labels—unless you're attending one of the Fashion Week shows at the Lincoln Centre (and even then it's better to hide your outfits' provenance in the style of Miuccia Prada). People here prefer a quieter existence, and that goes for their clothes, too. SoHo it's not.

In fact, Fashion Week regulars such as Grace Coddington, Creative Director of *Vogue* magazine, are perfect examples of the classic UWS aesthetic (even though Coddington lives downtown). Here it's black on black on black, with a little more black, all of which is then set off with a few ravishing pieces of jewellery and a great handbag—as the women in Ari Seth Cohen's *Advanced Style* blog often illustrate. The look here is minimalist, classic and coolly elegant. As one local quipped: 'We like being elegant but we also like being comfortable!', no doubt alluding to all those downtowners

who have a habit of wearing killer heels and clothes that dip and cling. This neighbourhood is where the highbrow, bookish, intelligentsia crowd like to hang out. (The book-focused film *You've Got Mail*, with Tom Hanks and Meg Ryan, was firmly set in this part of New York. That alone should give you an idea of the kind of area it is.) And—just like many members of the fashion, architecture and design set—the literary crowd likes its dark colours. Black, navy and grey have gravitas. Let the Upper East Side wear yellow and pink.

STAY: The Empire Hotel Oh, how I love the Empire! It's almost as good as NoMad, Crosby Street and Gramercy Park for style and service. Perhaps it's even on a level with them. It features a high-glam interior that's less UWS and more Hollywood. Picture a tangerine and chocolate colour palette with gilt and zebra prints—it's wild, but it works. But it's not the interior design that guests return for: it's the service. Staff here are so impeccable, you can't fault anything. When

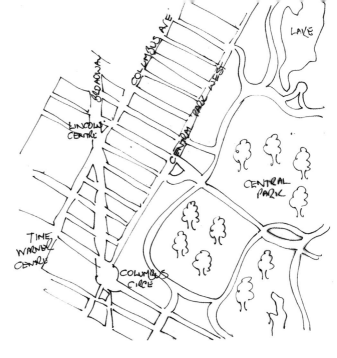

I stayed they kindly gave me an upgrade to an enormous suite, for free. I would return in a heartbeat. The hotel is also loved by fashion writers, and tends to be used as an impromptu office by international editors and bloggers during Fashion Week. In fact, The Empire's iconic glowing neon sign atop the rooftop terrace is often the backdrop for swanky parties by designers and media people. The hotel's 420 guestrooms are small, but if you politely ask for an upgrade, you might just get it. *44 West 63rd Street. www.empirehotelnyc.com*

DRINK: NYLO The rooms of the newly renovated/re-opened NYLO hotel have caused a bit of a stir with hotel and design fans, decorated as they are around a roaring twenties theme. (Very on-trend.) Some even have furnished balconies and views of Central Park and the Hudson River. (For those who miss out, there is also a shared balcony with the same vista.) But besides the rooms, the bar is where it's at here. A handsome, vintage-inspired

cocoon of tufted, chocolate-toned leather seats and a zinc bar that harks back to the hotel's 100-year-old history, it's as much of a pleasure zone as the NYLO's other swanky guest spaces, which include a 1920s French elevator system and a lobby where an in-house pianist tickles the ivories in the evenings. *2178 Broadway at West 77th Street. www.nylohotels.com*

TRIVIA

In the TV series *Will and Grace*, Will lived at 155 Riverside Drive. In *30 Rock*, Tina Fey's character, Liz Lemon, lived at 160 Riverside Drive. In *Seinfeld*, Jerry Seinfeld's character lived at 129 West 81st Street. And in *Sex and the City*, Charlotte lived at 275 Central Park West, while Miranda lived at 250 West 85th Street. All on the Upper West Side.

DINE: Ed's Chowder House inside the **Empire Hotel** is a pretty eatery where the décor is a fusion of chocolate, citrus and white, with stripes to add extra punch. It's no wonder it has become a firm fave with celebs and the fashion crowd. *Elle* magazine creative director, Joe Zee, and model Elettra Wiedemann (Isabella Rossellini's daughter) both adore it. Don't be shocked if, when you're having lunch or dinner, you recognise people from the worlds of television and/or publishing. *44 West 63rd Street. www.empirehotelnyc.com*

DINE: Caffè Storico (pictured this page) is a relatively new kid on the New York block. This cheery little cafe is hidden away in the New York Historical Society (storico is Italian for 'historic'). The lemon-and-white colour scheme is refreshingly different from anything else in the city, but it's the displays that really make guests smile. The walls are lined with enormous, 15-foot-high, chalky white, Victorian-style timber cabinets; the perfect backdrop to show off dozens of nineteenth-century china pieces from the museum's collection. It almost looks like a huge butler's pantry, or the servery of an enormous manor house, blown up to five times the size. UWS locals love it. The food is fab, too, and the service is always prompt and friendly. Afterwards you can peruse the extraordinary documents of the Historical Society next door— although the cafe is the real treasure here. *170 Central Park West. www.nyhistory.org*

WANDER: Riverside Park was made famous by its appearance in the film *You've Got Mail* (the 91st Street Garden within Riverside was the setting for the final scene), and it's just as enchanting in real life. There's a place at 105th Street where you can grab a beer and a burger inside the park—a great thing to do on a late summer afternoon—but all of the park is pleasurable. The film didn't lie: it really is that pretty. *Riverside Drive. www.nycgovparks.org*

EXPLORE: Pomander Walk is an enthralling and somewhat secret, English village-style neighbourhood that's hidden between Broadway and West End Avenue. It was inspired in 1910 by a Broadway play of the same name, although it's also

reminiscent of the row of mews houses near Washington Square Park. Many New Yorkers would have walked right by the stone wall and gated entrance and thought nothing of it, not suspecting that beyond lay a quaint narrow street of twenty-seven Tudor-style homes that seem to have been preserved in time. The street is full of whimsical architectural elements, such as decorative stucco, brick, painted wood trims, half-timber façades, painted wood shutters and flower window boxes. Some look like single-home cottages from the outside, with single-leaf painted wood doors, when they are actually two apartments one above the other. One of New York's true secrets. *Between West 94th Street and 95th Street, and Broadway and West End Avenue.*

Caffè Storico, at the New York Historical Society.

Opposite from top right, clockwise: taxi-yellow tulips in Central Park, a bold book cover by New York lover Cecil Beaton, New York-themed clutches and shoes at Kate Spade on the UWS, and taxi wellingtons for a wet day.

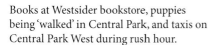

Books at Westsider bookstore, puppies being 'walked' in Central Park, and taxis on Central Park West during rush hour.

Opposite: The Empire Hotel.

FASHION, STYLE AND DESIGN DESTINATIONS

BLUEMERCURY Ever since 'hip' neighbourhoods like Brooklyn have become too pricy, ambitious retailers have been searching for the 'hot new spot' in New York. A surprising number of new businesses are setting up shop in the Upper West Side, and one of them is high-end apothecary chain Bluemercury. This chic cosmetics and beauty boutique has opened a 1700-square-foot store where the UWS's yummy mummies and beautiful bohos are. The products are so lovely you'll inevitably leave with more than you intended. Come here to refurbish your bathroom (or toiletry/travel bag) in style. *2305 Broadway. www.bluemercury.com*

BOC The UWS doesn't have as many cutting-edge designers as downtown, mostly because shoppers here tend to err on the side of conservative-chic, but there are a few boutiques serving up innovative and creative outfits, and this is one of them. It's the kind of place you'd expect to find in Brooklyn, frequented by stylistas searching for edgy labels. Brands range from cults, such as T by Alexander Wang and Inhabit to J Brand, to emerging names (Of Two Minds, Rozae Nichols) and established labels like Vivienne Westwood and Robert Rodriguez. The store also offers a free personal shopping service—bring in items you already own and the staff will pair them with superb clothes, shoes and accessories to send you on your merry way. According to *New York Magazine* the name BOC once stood for Boutique on Columbus, and even though the store has moved to Broadway (between 77th Street and 78th Street), the catchy moniker still stands. Sleek, chic and easy to deal with: just what you want in a New York boutique. *2191 Broadway. www.bocnyc.com*

COLUMBUS AVENUE AND COLUMBUS CIRCLE Columbus Avenue offers no surprises but it still holds lots of delights. Both sides of the streets, from 66th Street to about 86th Street, are dotted with good shops. Further south, there's Columbus Circle, where the stores are concentrated into an upscale mall for ease. All the usual grand brands are there— J Crew, Sephora, Williams-Sonoma, Sisley, Coach, Hugo Boss, Thomas Pink, Bose and a huge Whole Foods Market. However, there are also a few cuties tucked among the big names, such as FACE Stockholm, the Sisley part of Benetton (which offers gorgeous and quite covetable resort-style alternatives to Benetton's ubiquitous lines) and Aveda— always good for great shampoos. *10 Columbus Circle. www.theshopsatcolumbuscircle.com*

GREENFLEA MARKET The Greenflea Market in Brooklyn is widely recognised as being a great day out, but its UWS sibling is lesser known. The emphasis here is on antiques and vintage decorative goods and accessories, rather than food (although there are a few food stalls), and some of the offerings on display are surprising. For example, there's a lady who sells vintage teacups and saucers, which many aesthetes are now starting to collect. Many of the stalls sell, well, junk, but others offer great pieces, such as 1920s handbags and purses. There's even a man who sells Hermès on consignment. It's not a place you'd make a special trip for, but if you're in the area, it's a pleasant wander. *100 West 77th Street. www.greenfleamarkets.com*

INTERMIX The concept of two brothers who wanted a store where fashion lovers could browse high-end labels in one company, Intermix has been so successful since it opened in 1993 that the brothers have opened four more New York locations. It's a lovely example of how the Upper West Side likes to do things: quietly and with style. Many luxury European and American fashion brands, such as Chloé, DVF and Michael Kors are stocked, along with newer labels. There are only a few items of each line but the collections are well curated, and the store is so popular that sales are high and stock turnover is fast. *210 Columbus Avenue. www.intermixonline.com*

JOHN KOCH ANTIQUES This store is much like the rest of the UWS: it looks neat and sweet, but peek inside and it's a different story. The store's stock shifts so fast that it has a kind of market atmosphere, with displays and products being constantly moved, or packed up ready to go to clients, only to be replaced by new items arriving from auctions and estate sales. *Gotham Magazine* voted it 'the best treasure trove in Manhattan', and *The Good Wife* television show uses the store to source many of its set pieces. *201 West 84th Street. www.kochantiques.com*

MINT The name is as cute as the store. Mint is a girlie boutique, that's for sure, but it's not so tizzy that minimalists will feel the shudders. Mint's aesthetic is more gently feminine than froufrou. There are dressy pieces by great labels such as Minkpink and Dolce Vita footwear but there is also Mint's own house line of silk skirts and dresses. Add gorgeous gemstone jewellery by Jeanne Ruland, handbags by Tano (both designers creating pieces exclusively for the store) and other well-priced merch, and you have the perfect one-stop shop for ladylike style. *448 Columbus Avenue. www.shopmint.com*

OLDE GOOD THINGS Billed as an antique furniture store, Olde Good Things (love the quirky name) is more than that. It's an enormous jumble of gorgeous goods where you're likely to find things you've never seen before—and things you'll want to buy instantly, even if you have no immediate use for them. There are also a few Olde Good Things downtown but this Upper West Side one has nabbed a great location—right near the Natural History Museum and beautiful Central Park West buildings, where, I might add, it looks right at home. The store carries vintage pieces, antiques and great reproductions of old pieces, but it's the eclectic stuff that really turns heads. Designers often go there for heavy gilded doorknobs, for example (including those similar to the ones you find in Paris).

There are also beautiful old doors, house numbers, garden ornaments and a range of incredible statement pieces for your home. *450 Columbus Avenue. www.ogtstore.com*

TANI FASHIONABLE UWS ladies love this shoe store because it carries flats that don't look ugly or grannyish, or even flat-ish, but utterly glamorous. The store's owners source the prettiest shoes from around the world, from classic Bensimons to Chie Mihara boots, plus beautiful dress shoes and even snappy sneakers for wearing with jeans on weekends in Central Park or the Hamptons. There's also a back room for sale items that are marked up to 70 per cent off. New York is known as a mecca for shoe lovers and this store proves it. *2020 Broadway. www.tanishoes.com*

THÉRAPIE When it comes to those old-fashioned, apothecary-style pharmacies, no city does it better than New York. These range from truly authentic old stores (the iconic CO Bigelow; the oldest apothecary-pharmacy in the United States, founded in 1838) to stylish replicas. Thérapie is one of the latter, but it does merchandising like the old-timers. It's a three-storey emporium devoted to beauty, health, well-being and, well, everything that's scented, lovely and designed to lift you up, from upscale grooming products like Mason Pearson brushes, to racks of Spanx and Hue hosiery. There's also an entire mezzanine devoted to the, er, décolletage, from stay-put tape to delicately pretty bra straps. Catherine Zeta-Jones and Dustin Hoffman are regulars, among many. *309 Columbus Avenue. www.therapieny.com*

WESTSIDER In the film *You've Got Mail,* the bookshop belonging to Meg Ryan's character slowly folds due to the arrival of a highly branded, monolith-sized bookstore nearby. Well, thankfully there are still some lovely small bookstores left on the Upper West Side. Westsider is one. The favourite bookshop of many locals, Westsider is a teeny store, barely bigger than the books it sells, but oh, what atmosphere. There's a little bit of everything, from used titles to hard-to-find tomes. The books are piled high and the selection is always interesting. There are also some real gems at about half the cover price, including photography titles, art books and cookbooks. And if you have a special interest, no matter how unusual or quirky it might be, the staff will happily help you source books in that subject. The best kind of bookshop. *2246 Broadway. www.westsiderbooks.com*

ZABAR'S Most people know of Zabar's and its fabulous food, but few realise there is a great homewares section on the second floor. This being Zabar's, the kitchenware is particularly unbelievable. *2245 Broadway. www.zabars.com*

TIPS FROM AN INSIDER

NEW YORK MUSEUMS
LOVED BY
NEW YORKERS

Tricia Foley
Author and designer
www.triciafoley.com

Museum of the City of New York
1220 Fifth Avenue.
www.mcny.org

New York Historical Society
170 Central Park West.
www.nyhistory.org

Tenement Museum
103 Orchard Street.
www.tenement.org

Brooklyn Museum
200 Eastern Parkway.
www.brooklynmuseum.org

Donald Judd Museum
101 Spring Street.
www.juddfoundation.org

Metropolitan Museum of Art (Period Rooms)
1000 Fifth Avenue.
www.metmuseum.org

The Noguchi Museum
9–01 33rd Road.
www.noguchi.org

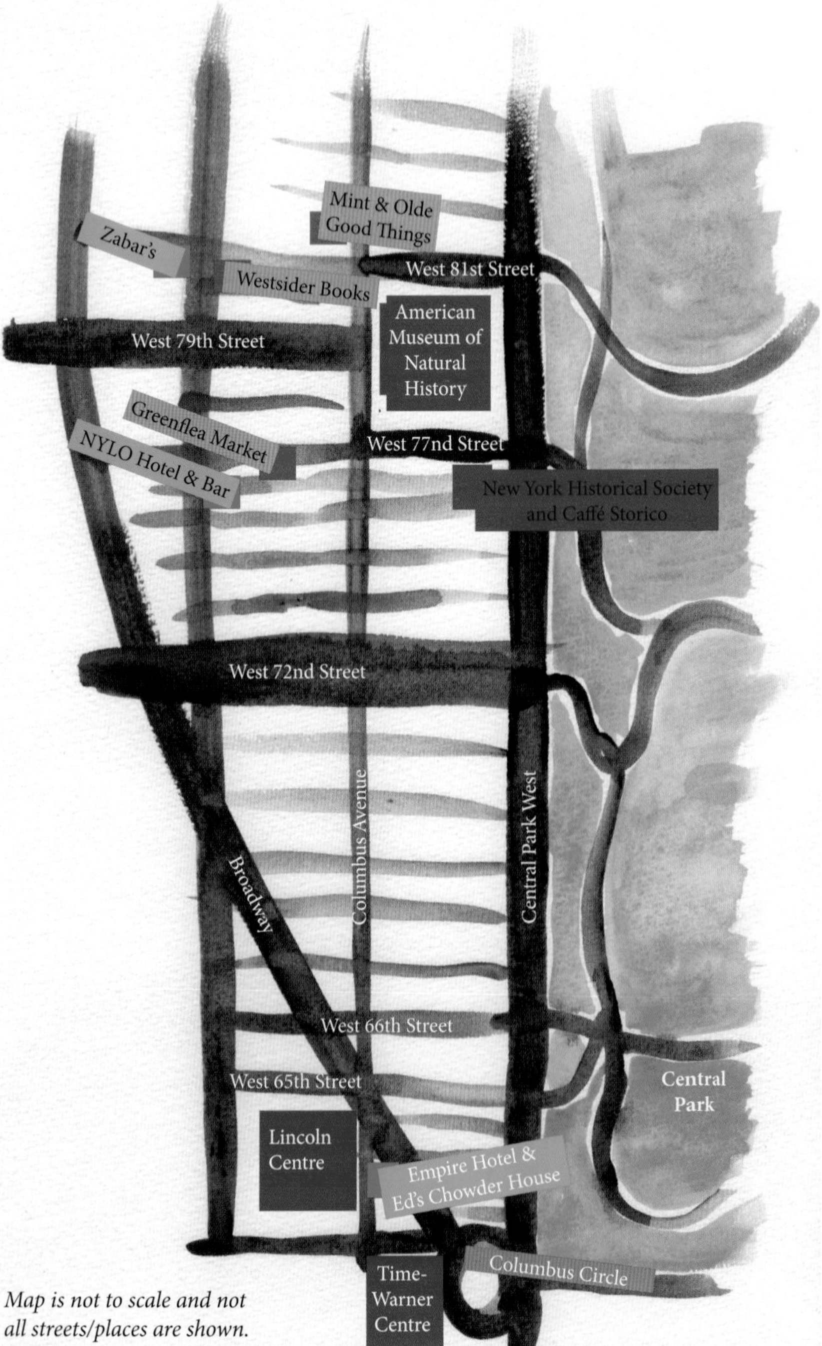

Zabar's

Mint & Olde
Good Things

West 81st Street

Westsider Books

West 79th Street

American
Museum of
Natural
History

Greenflea Market

West 77nd Street

NYLO Hotel & Bar

New York Historical Society
and Caffé Storico

West 72nd Street

Broadway

Columbus Avenue

Central Park West

West 66th Street

West 65th Street

Central
Park

Lincoln
Centre

Empire Hotel &
Ed's Chowder House

Map is not to scale and not
all streets/places are shown.

Time-
Warner
Centre

Columbus Circle

The Empire Hotel.
Opposite: A vintage mannequin at Olde Goode Things.

TIPS FROM AN INSIDER
NEW YORK ARCHITECTURAL GEMS

Steve Schappacher and Rhea White
Schappacher White Architects
www.schappacherwhite.com

There are so many things to love in New York that it's really hard
to narrow it down to a few, but here are some of our favorite
architectural spots.

The Smallpox Hospital, otherwise known as the Renwick Ruins.
Roosevelt Island. www.rihs.us/landmarks/renwick

The Grand Central Oyster Bar
Lower level, Grand Central Terminal, 89 East 42nd Street.
www.oysterbarny.com

The Noguchi Museum
9–01 33rd Road, Long Island. www.noguchi.org

And all the little tucked-away mews, backhouses and carriage houses.
We love the juxtaposition of scale, and the tiny islands of tranquillity
hidden within the hustle and bustle of the city.

TIPS FROM AN INSIDER

A DAY IN THE LIFE OF A NEW YORKER

Amy Parlow
New York Make-up Artist
www.amyparlowmakeup.com

My favorite museum in New York City is the **Museum of Modern Art.** I get so much creative inspiration by spending an afternoon there. *11 West 53rd Street. www.moma.org*

I then like to walk up to **Central Park** and get in some much needed time in nature. It's also great for people-watching.

From Central Park I'll walk over to **Barney's New York** and feel like a kid in a candy shop in their basement full of the best brands in makeup! *660 Madison Avenue. www.barneys.com*

A late lunch, early dinner at **Serafina Always** is next. I love their Farfalle Al Limoncello (bow tie pasta with shrimp, lemon zest, lemon juice and a touch of cream!) *33 East 61st Street. www.always.serafinarestaurant.com*

And to finish the day it's great to take in a film at **The Paris Theatre** which is next door to **The Plaza Hotel** on the corner of Fifth Avenue and Central Park. It's such a lovely venue and they always have a great selection of films. *4 West 58th Street. www.theparistheatre.com*

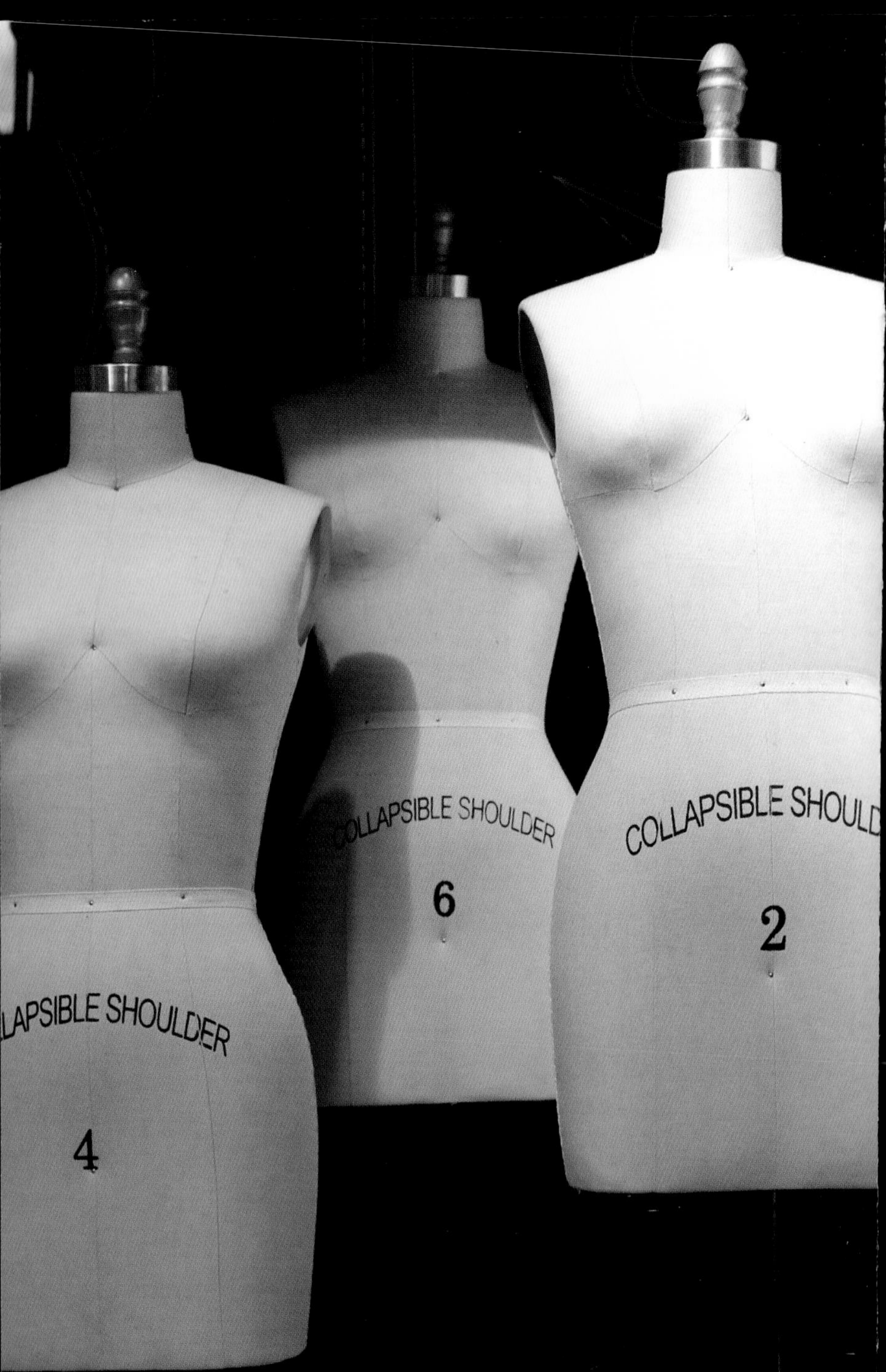
COLLAPSIBLE SHOULDER
6
COLLAPSIBLE SHOULD
2
LAPSIBLE SHOULDER
4

GARMENT DISTRICT AND BRYANT PARK

New York's
Sartorial and Literary Heart

Garment District & Bryant Park

*One's life and passion may be elsewhere, but New York is where you prove
if what you think in theory makes sense in life.*
—Miuccia Prada

The Garment District, also known as the Fashion District, is New York's sartorial heart. It's where many of New York's major fashion collections are born and where a designer's name can be made on the strength of a few well-cut patterns. The streets here are bursting at the seams with up-and-coming couturiers looking for that perfect bolt of fabric, design assistants searching for that unique button, retailers jostling for remnants left over from the end of designers' collections, and fashion students sourcing ideas and inspiration for their college projects. There is so much energy here in this concentration of fashion fabulousness that it often feels like a real-life catwalk show. Just without the camera-toting paparazzi.

The Garment District has been regarded as the centre for American fashion manu-facturing and fashion design since the early twentieth century. Some people think it's even the centre of the international fashion scene, but Italy, Paris and London remain strong competitors. What is evident is that fashion here is taken very, very seriously. Locals on the Upper East Side and in SoHo and the West Village may know their Thakoons from their Valentinos, but in the Fashion District they know their toiles like the backs of their hands. The neighbourhood—which is generally considered to sit between Fifth Avenue and 9th Avenue, from 34th to 42nd Street—is home to the majority of New York's fashion showrooms, and includes businesses such as Carolina Herrera, Oscar de la Renta, Calvin Klein and Donna Karan. And while the manufacturing has declined over the past two decades, there is still a lot of business being done—billions of dollars, in fact.

The Garment District is mainly a wholesale and trade area, rather than a retail

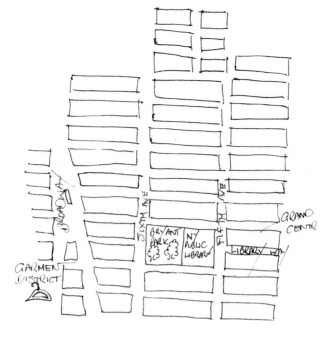

environment; however, if you're an ordinary consumer you can still purchase from many of the stores. In fact, most of the fabric and trimming places are filled with home sewers stockpiling discount fabrics. It's the equivalent of a candy store for fabric lovers and you do have to be careful you don't over-buy in the face of such enormous range and such low prices!

In the middle of all this fabric frenzy is Bryant Park, a pocket of leafy botanical calm amid a flurry of coloured fabric selvedges. It may look like a quiet respite from the sartorial madness of the streets around it, but the park still sees its share of fashion action. For a while, the semi-annual New York Fashion Week shows were held here, before they moved uptown to the Lincoln Centre for Performing Arts, and there are still many fashion events scheduled in the park each year.

But it's not just fashion that's celebrated here. Books are also lauded in this neighbourhood, which is not surprising when you realise that at one end of Bryant Park is the New York Public Library. This magnificent ode to the printed page opened in 1912, and is so large that some of the library stacks are actually under the park. The front steps of the library, including the sculpted lions, Patience and Fortitude, are officially part of Bryant Park, but the library's hushed calm is a world away from the playful mood of the shady space behind it. And if you're really dedicated to words and stories, you can follow Library Way to the Library Hotel for a drink, reading the witty literary plaques along the way.

Fashion and books, and a serene green space right in the heart of it all: what more could you possibly want from a neighbourhood?

STAY: A modern Manhattan hideaway created from a former millinery factory, the **Refinery Hotel** is perfectly placed for fashion and fabric shopping. The best part is that the interior features remnants of the old factory, including desks fashioned from old sewing machines. Another good alternative is **The Bryant Park Hotel.** This neo-gothic 23-storey skyscraper was designed for the American Radiator Company and features black brickwork and gold leaf in a truly glamorous piece of New York architecture that soars to the sky. It's also as full of drama inside, from all the flamboyant celebrity guests, as it is on the outside. *Refinery: 63 West 38th Street. www.refineryhotelnewyork.com; Bryant Park: 40 West 40th Street. www.bryantparkhotel.com*

DRINK: The somewhat secret **Campbell Apartment,** Grand Central Station, is tucked away above the station. It's the former private office of early twentieth-century tycoon John W Campbell, which has now been converted into an elegant bar that retains much of Campbell's sumptuously decorated interior. Although sumptuous is perhaps too understated a word for this space. The 'office' was originally designed to resemble a thirteenth-century Florentine palace, with a hand-painted plaster of Paris ceiling, leaded windows, a grand mahogany balcony, and a Persian carpet that took up the entire floor and cost $300 000, or roughly $3.5 million in today's money. There was also a permanent butler named Stackhouse (love the name). When the owner died, it became a jail, albeit a rather upscale one. However, in 1999, it was restored to its former glory and opened to the public to enjoy Campbell-level luxury. (The original steel safe is still there, as a reminder of Mr Campbell's wealth.) The space was recently spruced up by British designer Nina Campbell (no relation), who did it in twenty-four hours so the place didn't have to close. *Central Terminal, off the West Balcony, 15 Vanderbilt Avenue. www.grandcentralterminal.com*

BE INSPIRED: The Museum of the International Centre of Photography is a must for photography lovers. It always has good exhibitions, but the main reason for going is the fantastic gift store. I'm always buying cute gifts here—books, mobile/cell phone holders that look like Leica cameras, key rings with tiny cameras on them (complete with working flashes), charming journals and notebooks. The store is a real New York find. *1133 Avenue of the Americas (6th Avenue) at 43rd Street. www.icp.org*

ARCHITECTURAL TRAIL TO TAKE: As easy to miss as a good book in a crowded bookstore, **Library Way** is a little slice of gentle wisdom on the streets of New York. It runs along East 41st Street, between Fifth Avenue and Park Avenue, but if you approach from the east at Park, you'll have a perfect view of the grand entrance of the New York Public Library while you read the sidewalk snippets. There are ninety-six bronze plaques in total, each bearing lovely quotations from leading writers, such as Mark Twain, Albert Camus and Dylan Thomas. *East 41st Street, between Fifth Avenue and Park Avenue.*

*In the reading room
in the New York Public Library,
all sorts of souls were bent over
reading the past,
or the present,
or maybe it was the future,
patrons devoted to silence
and the flowering of
the imagination ...*

Richard Eberhart, Reading Room: the New York Public Library
(inscribed on a plaque on Library Way)

BENEFACTORS
1948 – 1958

HELENE HÖTLER CHENOLL
THOMAS W. LAMONT
MARY C. BROMBELL
LUCIUS WILMERDING
THE VINCENT ASTOR FOUNDATION
THE CHANGE FOUNDATION INC. NEW YORK
THE ROCKEFELLER FOUNDATION
MARY S. KOROLOFF
ENID CHAMBERS HUMPHREYS
MORRIS HADLEY
H. DUNSCOMBE COLT
LILY D. PULITZER
CARL H. PFORZHEIMER
LOUIS MARTIN
EMMA DEAN SIPPER
MORTIMER AND ANNA WARREN
CLEVELAND H. DODGE FOUNDATION INC.
JOHN R. SLATTERY
MABEL HERBERT HARPER
LATHROP COLGATE HARPER

Recollection

SEE: Many tourists head for the top of the Empire State Building for sky-high views of Manhattan, but the **Top of The Rock** (the Rockefeller Center) is just as good—and the queues are far shorter than its more famous neighbour. While the Empire's vistas include downtown and the Flatiron, the Rock's actually include the Empire State, so you can shoot it from above, as well as Central Park on the other side. Both scenes make for great photographs when the sun goes down and the twilight loveliness descends on Manhattan's iconic skyline. *30 Rockefeller Plaza. www.topoftherocknyc.com*

The *glamour* of *it all!*

—*Charlie Chaplin*

FASHION, STYLE
AND DESIGN DESTINATIONS

ANNE FONTAINE The white shirt is a staple in many a stylista's wardrobe, and those in the know buy theirs at Anne Fontaine. This French label has been supplying the world's most glamorous women with their white shirts for years. And, being French, these sartorial classics are a little different from the standard cuff-collar-and-button style. Some have enormous sleeves that puff up in a truly glamorous fashion. Others are fitted to emphasise the bust. And others are just showpieces on their own. All you need is a pair of black pants and you're done! *610 Fifth Avenue. www.annefontaine.com*

ANTHROPOLOGIE I once saw Anthropologie's interior described as 'Fez-meets-Florence'. It made me laugh because it's spot on. You've never seen a more haute-bohemian space. There are frocks that look vintage but are new, and homewares that look roughed up but are also new. In fact, there are seemingly endless amounts of gypsy-ish clothing, and vintage-style accessories and homewares. Somehow it all looks great, possibly thanks to the merchandising, which is always clever. There's also a whole lot of fantastic kitchenalia and hardware (cute door knobs, for example), plus gorgeous new books and classic bathroom décor. (The ruffled white shower curtains were a huge seller one year.) You, too, will be seduced by Anthropologie's cheeky charm. *50 Rockefeller Plaza. www.anthropologie.com*

BANANA REPUBLIC I know wealthy women who come here each year to top up their preppy wardrobes. Banana Republic, you see, does preppy as well as the expensive brands but at one-quarter of the price. This store, at the Rockefeller Center, is particularly chic, with Art Deco details and three huge floors featuring everything from covetable bags to cute dresses. There are always classics here, too, such as those three perennial favourites: beige pants, white linen shirts and pretty pearls. *626 Fifth Avenue. www.bananarepublic.com*

GRAY LINE LINEN There are dozens of fabric stores in the Garment District (just wander around: you'll stumble across them everywhere), but my favourites are Mood, Rosen & Chadick and Gray Line Linen.

In the latter, as you can tell by the name, linen is king. If you're a fan of this cool, elegant fabric—whether in homewares or clothes—this is the place to come. Colours veer on the subdued side—think sophisticated greys, beiges and creamy whites—but it's still a feast for the senses. The textures alone are incredible. No nasty cheap stuff here! A lot of decorators use this store to source vintage-looking linens to re-upholster old chairs and sofas. Personally, I love the range of white linens: perfect for summer shirts and frocks. *260 West 39th Street. www.graylinelinen.com*

HYMAN HENDLER & SONS This store is one of the best in the city for ribbons: the selection is always interesting. Hyman's specialty is vintage ribbons and trims, so if you're looking for something to finish off a wedding gown (something old; something new), prettify a summer frock, add an elegant touch to the wrapping of a special gift or enhance a Cecil Beaton/*My Fair Lady*–style hat for the races or a wedding, this is the store to source it from. Many of the products are designed and handmade especially for Hyman Hendler by mills in France, Italy and Switzerland. The materials range from cotton to rayon, silk, satin, linen, wool, taffeta and velvet. However, the ribbons most people come here for are the delightful vintage grosgrains, jacquards and brocades. My favourite are the stripes—very South of France. *21 West 38th Street. www.hymanhendler.com*

J. CREW This is an almost cult-ish label. This is because the company's creative head, Jenna Lyons, has transformed the brand from a preppy Nantucket/New England–style label to an edgier look that mixes high brow with street style, and sequined glamour with nerdy androgyny. Some bloggers even admit to being 'obsessed' with Jenna Lyons' life and J. Crew's collections. While I'm not as enamoured with J. Crew as many; nonetheless I can see the appeal. Like any great US fashion label (Ralph Lauren, Kate Spade), J. Crew has become more than just clothes; it has become an entire lifestyle. And what I love about the stores, particularly the one in the Rockefeller Center, is that there's more than just fashion on offer: there are also vintage books (I've seen a signed CZ Guest book here for $250) and other witty ephemera for sale. Even the interior and fittings are fascinating (the Serge Mouille light fixtures, for example). The best section, however, is the sale section at the rear of the stores, where you can often find gorgeous shoes and dresses marked way down. Recently, the company has revamped their catalogues (a recent shoot was done at Amanda Brooks' stylish country house in England), and the company seems to be going from (fashion) strength to (fashion) strength. *30 Rockefeller Center. www.jcrew.com*

LIBRARY HOTEL Inspired by its proximity to the New York Public Library, just one block away, the Library Hotel was one of the first library-inspired hotels in the world. (There are now many; in recent years they've popped up like paperbacks at an airport bookshop.) It's a sublime place if you love books, and even if you don't, it's still a lovely place to stay. Rooms are organised according to the Dewey decimal system, so you can request your subject matter and indulge in books on that topic supplied in the complimentary pile beside the bed. (I love the Architecture Room.) The hotel has a collection of more than 6000 books, and those that aren't in the rooms and suites are in the lobby (which itself looks like a library) or upstairs in the cosy public reading areas. One of the upstairs areas has a fireplace and a bar, perfect for winter nights in, while the rooftop terrace is hugely popular with locals on summer nights. *299 Madison Avenue. www.libraryhotel.com*

M&J TRIMMING You can't miss this store: just look for the enormous sign. Then again, most serious seamstresses and haberdashery devotees already know the location: M&J's has long been a go-to spot

for that hard-to-find beading or ribbon trim. It's an extensive store, with a well-displayed layout and lovely staff (who are incredibly patient). The collections cover buttons, braids, ribbons, beads, leather bits, feathers and even handbag handles—just the thing for making that bamboo-handled, Hermès-style number. *1008 6th Avenue. www.mjtrim.com*

MACY'S If you feel intimadated venturing into Saks Fifth Avenue, Henril Bendel, Bergdorf Goodman or any other upscale store uptown, this place might be more your style. Macy's is designed for the common man, but its interior and products are far from common. Once the largest department store in the world for many years, it's always been something of an icon in this city (the annual Macy's Thanksgiving Day Parade is famous), and since its recent renovation it has emerged bright and inviting again. Some shoppers hate the crowds here; others like the affordable product ranges. I found the interior to be surprisingly chic, and was able to get in, buy a new handbag in a hurry (to replace one that had broken) and get out again without much trouble. If you want to tackle the upper floors, perhaps go at odd times to lessen the impact of the crowds. Service can be hit and miss, but the accessories and fashion is well worth a browse if you're on a budget. *151 West 34th Street.* *www.macys.com/newyork*

MOOD FABRICS If you're a fabric lover, there's one store in the world you must see: Mood. Most seamstresses are accustomed to fabric stores that are fairly small— the exception being the stores in Paris' Montmartre district. So the first sight of this emporium can come as something of a shock. It's huge: three enormous floors stacked to the ceiling with fabrics. Newbies tend to spend an hour or more doing one floor and then realise, with a gulp, there are two more to go, and they've not left enough time. I warn you: you'll need a few hours here. Many of the bolts come from high-end designers who ordered too much for their collections. Other fabrics are remnants or discontinued lines. I've bought Ralph Lauren pinstripe linens here for $10, as opposed to the $200 they would normally be if you bought them from Ralph Lauren's own website. There's also a great online store, for when you can't fly to New York—and they ship internationally. I'm telling you: if you're into fabric, Mood is the mecca! *225 West 37th Street. www.moodfabrics.com*

NEW YORK ELEGANT FABRICS Okay, so the name isn't that imaginative, but the store makes up for it. If you want a good selection of wool, cashmere, linen, striped cotton, printed cotton, raw silk or indeed any other textiles, this is a good place to start. It can be a bit of a jumble in parts, as opposed to Rosen & Chadick's beautifully ordered aisles (see below), but if ye seek ye shall find. I discovered a dozen bolts of gorgeous leopard and other (fake) animal prints here: the perfect fabric to make a tufted ottoman. *222 West 40th Street. www.nyelegantfabrics.com*

ROSEN & CHADICK A more upmarket version of the more famous Mood Fabrics store around the corner, Rosen & Chadick is where many up-and-coming fashion designers, stylists and interior designers source their fabrics. It's tricky to find (the entrance is around the side), but you'll love it when you do. The double-level store is filled with high-end fabrics, including many remnants from designers such as Armani, who sell them when they've finished designing their collections. There are 125 linen colours alone. Leave plenty of time. *561 7th Avenue (2nd floor). www.rosenandchadickfabrics.com*

ZARA Oh, Zara. What can we say about this mega-store? Some fashion people dismiss it but you can't deny it's won over a larger part of the market. The key to Zara's success is that the stores look sophisticated (rather than a jumble sale, like H & M often do), and the company brings out collections that are so on-trend the styles, colours and silhouettes are on Zara's floors almost as soon as they've been seen on the fashion catwalks. Oh—and the prices are incredibly cheap, too. You can find great wardrobe basics here: navy woollen coats, sophisticated black dresses, smart business totes, easy white shirts, but what Zara does well is the quirky twist on the fashion classic. The problem is, the label is so popular that if you find something you like, you'd better buy it quick, as it's liable to sell out. New stock appears weekly, and turnover is high. This store, at Fifth Avenue, is particularly good, because it has enough space to breathe, unlike its congested cousin downtown. *500 Fifth Avenue. www.zara.com*

There are thousands of bolts of fabrics
in the Garment District, from tangerine
tweed to Schiaparelli-pink silk.
Opposite: Ribbons at M&J Trimming.

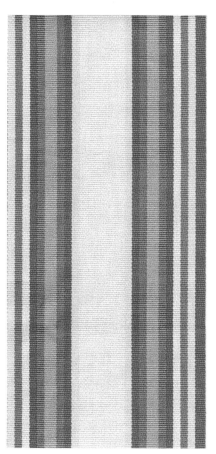

I like the gritty parts of fashion: the design, the studio, the pictures …

—Vera Wang

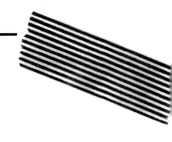

TIPS FROM AN INSIDER

Tricia Foley
Tricia Foley Design, New York
www.triciafoley.com

RESTAURANTS

BARBUTO Jonathan Waxman has created the perfect casual restaurant out of a converted garage on a quiet West Village street. The open kitchen has a wood-fired oven and serves up Californian-Italian fare. Tables and chairs spill out onto the street in summer. Always friendly, always delicious. *775 Washington Street. www.barbutonyc.com*
THE BAR ROOM AT THE MUSEUM OF MODERN ART (MoMA) Love the design, the buzz, the people and the food. There's also a great place to eat at the bar if you're on your own. *11 West 53rd Street. www.moma.org*
THE CITY BAKERY The perfect take-out place for breakfast or lunch. Maury Rubin has created a downtown mecca for those who love his baked goods, soups and salads. There is even a hot chocolate bar in winter! Great for a bite in between shopping or gallery-hopping downtown, or for meeting friends for a casual lunch or brunch. *3 West 18th Street. www.thecitybakery.com*
ABC KITCHEN All white and natural wood, with tables set with mix-and-match vintage china, ABC's scene is always bustling. The food by Jean Georges Vongerichten is all natural, but with a twist. *35 East 18th Street. www.abchome.com/eat/abc-kitchen*

SHOPS

TED MUEHLING From simple white porcelain cups to a modern silver tea strainer, the objects on sale here are always beautifully designed and displayed. *52 White Street. www.tedmuehling.com*
MUJI I get excited about the all-white swiffers and cleaning supplies, food containers, notebooks and organisers that: always beautiful and functional. My favourite place for chic household supplies. *620 8th Avenue. www.muji.us*
MOON RIVER CHATTEL A mix of old and new wares, including light fixtures, design books and linens, all filling up an old storefront in a historic section of Williamsburg, Brooklyn. *62 Grand Street. www.moonriverchattel.com*
ABC CARPET & HOME The linen department stocks all the best lines; the furniture department has unique vintage, mid-century modern and classics; and the tabletop downstairs is filled with artisanal pottery, wood serving-platters and other unique pieces. *888 and 881 Broadway. www.abchome.com*
AERO Brimming with my friend Thomas O'Brien's designs, from furniture, lighting, rugs and tabletops. *419 Broome Street. www.aerostudios.com*

Bryant Park Hotel

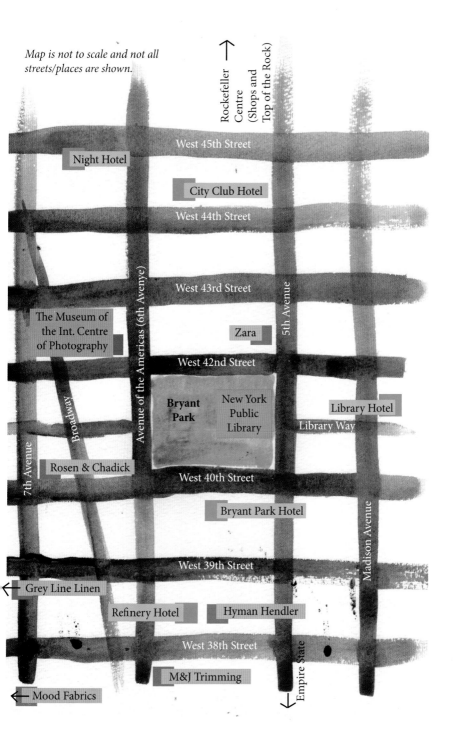

Map is not to scale and not all streets/places are shown.

Rockefeller Centre (Shops and Top of the Rock)

West 45th Street

Night Hotel

City Club Hotel

West 44th Street

West 43rd Street

5th Avenue

The Museum of the Int. Centre of Photography

Zara

West 42nd Street

Bryant Park

New York Public Library

Library Hotel

Library Way

Broadway

7th Avenue

Rosen & Chadick

West 40th Street

Bryant Park Hotel

Avenue of the Americas (6th Avenye)

Madison Avenue

West 39th Street

← Grey Line Linen

Refinery Hotel

Hyman Hendler

West 38th Street

Empire State

M&J Trimming

← Mood Fabrics

WANDER: Bryant Park is the best kind of park, in that, as well as being a leafy oasis amid the bustle of the Garment District, it's also an ode to leaves of another kind: the ones found in books. Yes, this park is a green and gracious tribute to writers and the written word.

The space was actually named after a poet, the editor and civic reformer William Cullen Bryant, who was the editor of the *New-York Evening Post* for more than fifty years. (Back then, it was more highbrow and less tabloid.) A statue of him is at the east end of Bryant Park, adjoining Bryant Park Grill. There are also statues of other noted literary names, including German writer Johann Wolfgang von Goethe (look for the bust that faces the carousel) and Gertrude Stein (near the Bryant Park Grill).

A great thing to do in Bryant Park over the summer months is go to one of the outdoor movies shown in Bryant Park on Monday nights in summer. Bring a rug and a picnic dinner, find a good spot on the lawn, and watch an old cinematic classic under the stars. *West 42nd Street, between Fifth Avenue and 6th Avenue. www.bryantpark.org*

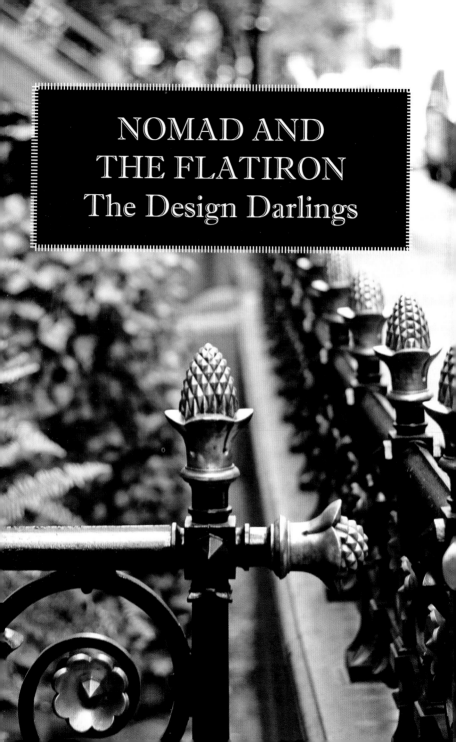

NOMAD AND THE FLATIRON
The Design Darlings

One of the big things I miss about New York is not my friends so much;
it's Shake Shack, the burger place. I miss Shake Shack.
—Aziz Ansari

The Flatiron area, named after the famous Flatiron Building that stands on a triangular island block formed by Fifth Avenue, Broadway and East 22nd Street, has long been top of the 'to do' list for international design lovers travelling to Manhattan. There's nothing else like this triangular, cheese grater–shaped building anywhere else in New York, indeed anywhere else on the design globe. And there's nothing else like the neighbourhood that surrounds it, either. It's an enclave of design houses, daring architecture (the Empire State, for one, which you can see from the Flatiron), photogenic streetscapes, and intriguing hotels, houses, bars, boutiques, homewares stores and other aesthetic delights. In short, the Flatiron is an extraordinarily creative quarter.

What's more, the creative presence of architecture, design, media and publishing companies has not only encouraged others to move into the area (see the list of newbies over), but introduced a whole new energy to the urban landscape. Danny Meyer's hugely popular Shake Shack in Madison Square Park is always bustling with life (especially on a sunny day when it feels like the queue stretches to Brooklyn), the streets are full of vivid window displays, and the cool and quirky bars and bistros overflow with the black-collar crowd working in creative industries. It's certainly a great place to explore if you're into design.

The Flatiron effect also flows out to neighbouring areas. The newly revived NoMad neighbourhood (named for North of Madison) is becoming just as innovative. Once a slightly grubby no-man's land full of grand but aging architecture and $2 stores, it has been re-energised by a couple of savvy developers. The Ace Hotel was first, turning a previously neglected street into a new destination for aesthetes with its startlingly hipster interior and come-and-play philosophy. And when the NoMad Hotel followed (by the same group), with its more upmarket Paris-meets-Manhattan

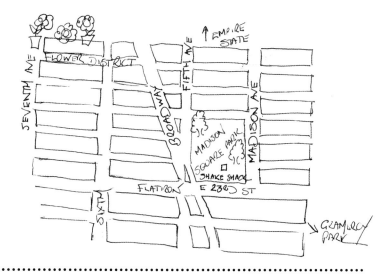

elegance wrapped up in a Beaux Arts building, well, there was no recognising the ol' hood! Both hotels soon attracted a slew of gorgeous stores and eateries, including Maison Kitsuné, the John Dory Oyster Bar, The Breslin, and those bars inside the hotels. (The cupola-topped rooftop of the NoMad is amazing in itself.)

A few blocks over, there's the Gramercy Park neighbourhood, which is yet another design lover's dream.

Whatever your passion—architecture, design, interior design, unusual design, iconic design—there is something here to inspire you. Welcome to one of the most inspirational design neighbourhoods in Manhattan.

DRINK: Andrew Zobler and the other creators behind **The Ace Hotel / The Breslin Bar and Dining Room** were some of the first to recognise that the NoMad neighbourhood was a wealth of raw, unrenovated, Beaux Arts loveliness, ripe for restoration. He decided to open an Ace Hotel there, and in doing so not only revived a previously neglected neighbourhood but also introduced a whole new aesthetic to New York. Think: Ralph Lauren meets Hogwarts school. The reception looks like the science lab, the foyer resembles a grand old hall of a private Scottish boarding school, complete with red tartan fabrics and bowls of cricket balls, and the rooms have the feel of a college dorm. Some appreciate it; others feel it's like going back to school. But the real appeal here is the bar: The Breslin Bar & Dining Room is one of the loveliest pubs in town. Created by the same foodies behind the hugely popular Spotted Pig in the West Village, The Breslin has a bold Kelly-green palette, plus a menu of top-nosh. It's casual, yet clever at the same time. *16 West 29th Street. www.thebreslin.com*

PHOTOGRAPH: The Flatiron.
The Chrysler and the Empire State buildings may steal the show on the stage that is New York's skyline, but one significantly smaller building remains a crowd favourite. It has an odd shape, an odder name and sits on an even odder site, but—like Sophia Loren—the mismatching parts add up to a spectacularly beautiful whole.

The Flatiron Building, originally called the Fuller Building, was—and still is—considered a groundbreaking skyscraper. Surprisingly, it was one of the tallest buildings in the city when it was finished in 1902, although now it's the small kid on the block. Yet despite its diminished presence (architecturally speaking), it still commands attention. You can't help but notice it as you stroll south down Broadway.

The building sits on a triangular island block formed by Fifth Avenue, Broadway and East 22nd Street. It's significant on the map because it acts as a kind of segue between the south (downtown) and the north (uptown). The Flatiron is where a New York shift takes place, both in a cartographic sense and a psychological one. It's also here that Broadway, which runs on a diagonal through the city, changes from being on the west to the east. The Flatiron's ship's bow-shaped apex acts somewhat like an ocean liner, changing the current.

The building is so loved by New Yorkers that many cite sitting in Madison Square Park on a sunny day as one of their favourite activities. (The park looks up at the Flatiron.) Even the building's tenants are fond of its awkward shape. When the employees of one of the publishing houses that rents several floors of the Flatiron were asked if they would like to upgrade to new offices elsewhere, they declined. (The 'point' offices are the most coveted in the building and feature amazing northern views that look directly upon the Empire State Building.)

Several years ago, in 2009, an Italian real estate investment firm bought a majority stake in the building with plans to turn it into a luxury hotel. Although some will lament the change, others will undoubtedly appreciate the opportunity to experience the Flatiron from inside as well as out. *175 Fifth Avenue*

RELAX: Danny Meyer's ingeniously casual **Shake Shack** in Madison Square Park (pictured) is always great, but always busy. If you can't be bothered waiting in line (you should see the queues some days), just sit on one of the Shake Shack's chairs or on a nearby park bench with a bottled water and watch New Yorkers at play. The park is an alluring pocket of greenery (there's an entertaining dog run), and if you can get to the Shake Shack, the food is great, too. *Between 23rd Street and 26th Street, and Madison Avenue and Fifth Avenue. www.shakeshack.com*

DINE: Eleven Madison Park is where you go if you love food and fancy spending big bucks on a memorable meal. It's considered one of New York's best restaurants and has a Michelin star to prove it. The most interesting dishes come when you choose the 'grid menu': you pick an ingredient and the chefs build your meal around it. Inspiring dining. *11 Madison Avenue. www.elevenmadisonpark.com*

EXPLORE: One of the most beautiful neighbourhoods in New York is that surrounding **Gramercy Park**, and the street New Yorkers call the 'Block Beautiful' is just that: extraordinarily beautiful. The block actually covers East 19th Street, between Irving Place and 3rd Avenue, but you can wander around anywhere here really and be rewarded with architectural eye candy. There are also some pretty glam residents—Karl Lagerfeld has an apartment here and Jennifer Aniston reportedly bought one but then decided not to stay in it because of all the media attention. (Note: Gramercy Park itself is a private park, meaning only local residents have the key. But if you stay at the Gramercy Park Hotel you have guest access.) *East 21st Street between Lexington Avenue and Irving Place.*

STROLL: The Gramercy Park Neighbourhood. I discovered Gramercy Park late in my New York education. I stumbled upon it when I checked into the legendary Gramercy Park Hotel, which was offering a special on their rooms (I could not have afforded it otherwise). What a fortuitous move. I checked in, and never wanted to leave again. Both the Gramercy Park Hotel and the timelessly beautiful village surrounding it are two of the most enthralling places in town.

The hotel is a dazzling snapshot of dramatic design (and often equally dramatic VIP guests) in an otherwise tranquil, tree-lined neighbourhood. But don't let the serenity fool you. This neighbourhood is alive with history and the spirits of New York legends. The Astors, Morgans, Rockefellers and Roosevelts all lived here, and their strikingly elegant townhouses are still part of the neighbourhood's unique appeal.

The Gramercy Park neighbourhood was one of the country's earliest examples of city planning. Created in the 1830s as a display of stately townhouses centred around a spectacular garden (Gramercy Park), it attracted a roll call of stellar residents, from Oscar Wilde to John Barrymore, James Cagney, John Steinbeck, Thomas Edison and the aforementioned dynasties. In recent times, it has lured Uma Thurman, Winona Ryder, Jimmy Fallon, Rufus Wainwright, Karl Lagerfeld and Jennifer Aniston. For a while, Katie Holmes lived around the corner.

While you can't enter Gramercy Park unless you're a resident of the apartments around it or a guest of the Gramercy Park Hotel, you can wander the streets of this dignified, distinguished area, which offers some of New York's most impressive architecture. Don't miss Stanford White's The Player's Club (*16 Gramercy Park South, www.theplayersnyc.org*), the National Arts Club—the former home of Governor Samuel Tilden (*15 Gramercy Park South, www.nationalartsclub.org)*, and 36 Gramercy Park East, a neo-Gothic fantasy of terracotta where gargoyles stand guard high over the greenery.

If you do stay at the Gramercy Park Hotel, ask the doorman or concierge for the key to the park. The serene, tree-lined oasis is the perfect place to find peace and quiet, read the paper or reflect on the neighbourhood's rich history. *Between East 20th and East 21st, and Irving Place and Lexington Avenue.*

Marimekko

Map is not to scale and not all streets/places are shown.

West 28th Street

East 24th Street

NoMad Hotel

West 27th Street

Park Avenue South

Broadway

West 26th Street

Madison Avenue

East 26th Street

Antiques Garage

5th Avenue

Madison Square Park

Avenue of the Americas

Eleven Madison Park

West 24th Street

Shake Shack

East 24th Street

Marimekko

Eataly

West 23rd Street

East 23rd Street

Flatiron Building

East 22nd Street

Union Square

East 21st Street

Club Monaco

Gramercy Park →

Kate Spade

WANDER: The Union Square Greenmarket is a sign that New York hasn't urbanised completely. Spread across Union Square on certain days (Monday, Wednesday, Friday and Saturday from 8 a.m. to 6 p.m.), it turns an otherwise ordinary city square into a rural arcadia. Stalls full of fresh produce overflow into one another, and on a sunny day the effect can be utterly delightful. Partly because of the market's success, the streets and boutiques surrounding Union Square have become popular with young professionals, designers and artists. *North and west sides of Union Square Park, East 14th Street and Broadway. www.grownyc.org/greenmarket*

STAY: The Jacques Garcia-designed interior of the **NoMad Hotel i**s unlike anything else in New York. In fact, it has more in common with Paris, or perhaps New Orleans. Garcia (who did Paris' Hôtel Costes) was inspired by the Paris apartment of his youth, but he also wanted to create a place that felt like a wealthy French person had moved to a grand residence in New York to start a new life. The rooms are little *Vogue Living*–style vignettes of opulent glamour, with upturned steamer trunks used as bars, and elegant folding screens instead of interior walls. However, it's the dining areas—the Library Bar, the Atrium and the Parlour— where the sophistication of Garcia's design really becomes apparent. Imagine swags of Champagne-coloured silk, velvet sofas and club chairs, a fireplace from a French château, a two-storey library with a 200-year-old spiral staircase to a mezzanine, and other nostalgic, luxurious touches. It's been a hit with New Yorkers ever since it opened in early 2013, and looks set to be a Manhattan classic. Another great little bolthole is the recently renovated **Roger New York** hotel. Tucked away just north of Madison Square Park, it's a wonderfully affordable option for people who care as much about style as they do price. The design features striped black-and-white awnings, a seductive foyer with petrol-blue chaises, old New York–style photos and a geranium green rug. The rooms, meanwhile, are sophisticated navy-blue retreats that are surprisingly large for a midtown hotel in Manhattan. Ask for one with a terrace: they're not that expensive and the luxury of walking outside to look over the streetscape is wonderful. *NoMad: 1170 Broadway. www.thenomadhotel.com; Roger New York: 131 Madison Avenue. www.therogernewyork.com*

Restoration Hardware (RH).
Opposite from top left: Fishs Eddy,
ABC Carpet & Home, the Union
Square Greenmarket and a 'find' at the
antiques markets around
West 25th Street.

FASHION, STYLE
& DESIGN DESTINATIONS

ABC CARPET & HOME Interior decorators and design lovers go slightly gaga when they enter this store, and I can understand why. It's a gorgeous, multi-storeyed emporium of unusual furniture, textiles, antiques, clothing, jewellery, bedding and décor. Everything here has character. And there are some great statement pieces. It's often visually exhausting but fab nonetheless. The rug department is especially notable, and includes designers like Madeline Weinrib (who has the most superbly coloured designs). For those who can't afford Ms Weinrib's high prices, the store also has a warehouse in the Bronx, where you can find some of the same designer goods at discounted prices. If you're into interior design or homewares, then your New York stay won't be complete without a wander through here. *888 and 881 Broadway (two stores opposite each other). www.abchome.com*

ACE HOTEL I stayed at the Ace as a journalist a week before it officially opened in order to shoot it for a book on hotels. It was noisy, and full of workman and debris. And my room, while spacious, was austere.

I couldn't work out what the media fuss was about. Then, at midnight, I decided to open my blind to see if the window would also open. That's when I saw the Empire State Building, right in front of my window, twinkling in the night sky. Then I knew. The Ace likes to keep it best cards up its sleeve. It likes to surprise its guests. Much of the charm of this place comes in the form of discovering its quirks. The entrance/reception/foyer/lounge/bar is an enormous space that features whimsical, science lab–style cabinets and quirky graffiti wallpaper. There are also super-comfy leather sofas to lounge around on and check your emails. Even the Stumptown café has been done with an old library feel, with baristas dressed in vintage chic. Some people like it; others sneer at its aesthetic. Whatever you feel about it, the Ace Hotel has certainly caused a scene. *20 West 29th Street. www.acehotel.com/newyork*

ANTIQUES GARAGE If you love searching for treasures among the trash, West 25th Street is the place to go. There are several flea and antique places in this area, and one of the most popular is the

Antiques Garage. It features two floors full of stalls selling eclectic antiques and vintage pieces, including fashion and decorative arts. There are paintings and prints, jewellery, handbags, fabrics, rugs, furniture, and every type of fine silver item imaginable. Some of the stalls to watch out for include Athena Vintage Clothing, Bill McCleen (vintage cameras), Bryce Thomas Antiques (Limoges and more), George's Collectibles (steamer trunks and other antiques), Kristine (antique, mid-century and modern design), Lali Antiques (silver, crystal, mirrors, paintings and furniture), Marlow's Treasure Chest (vintage signs), and Noel's Art and Antiques (paper ephemera such as photos, maps, documents and so on). There are also stalls selling industrial antiques, vintage textiles from India, silver, vintage clothing and costume jewellery. Open only on the weekend. *112 West 25th Street. www.hellskitchenfleamarket.com*

EATALY Launched by chef Mario Batali, this is a foodie's emporium of restaurants, cafés, stores, a cooking school and a rooftop restaurant. It sells almost every kind of food and produce you can imagine, from French to Russian, Italian and Polish. If you're starving, it's a dangerous place to go! There are all kinds of takeaway counters to choose from, including a bread bar and a meat bar. Warning: Once you go in you may never come out again, especially if you love all things related to flavour. *200 Fifth Avenue. www.eataly.com*

FISHS EDDY It's a crazy name and an even crazier store, filled to the rafters with dinnerware of all shapes, colours and sizes. Odd, maybe, but New Yorkers (and foreigners) love it. The twist is that this dinnerware is different from the usual fancy sets found uptown. There are plates with floorplans on them (great for architects), platters with New York Times crosswords, salt and paper shakers with silhouettes of skylines, and coffee cups with prints of all kinds of quirky New York images. It's completely mad, of course, but very New York. If you're not bold enough to buy a floorplan platter (the penthouse ones are fabulous), there are more subtle designs. And all sorts of kitchen things, too. A great store for gifts, or one to stop off at if you love cooking. *889 Broadway. www.fishseddy.com*

JEWEL DIVA Quite possibly one of the best sources of vintage Chanel in the world, Jewel Diva is at the New York Showplace. This site, in itself, is a jewellery box of extraordinary goods, but Jewel Diva is perhaps the best. It's a tiny stall, barely bigger than a Chanel earring, but the owner is clearly well connected when it comes to vintage designer jewellery—and clearly informed. You can tell she knows her stuff: the last time I visited she was carrying a lot of vintage Chanel pendant necklaces, which are very 'in' at the moment. She also stocks Dior and many other fine French jewellery pieces, some of which date back to the 1920s. Her tagline is 'From deco to disco, Victorian to modernist, Haskell to Chanel', which sums it up, really. If you don't see what you like, or want, just ask her (or her staff): they may have the perfect piece stored elsewhere. No wonder the fashion editors love her. One of New York's best-kept jewellery secrets. *40 West 25th Street, Galleries 8, 9 and 9a. www.jeweldiva.com*

MAISON KITSUNÉ This sleek boutique is the Manhattan outpost of the much-hyped and super-cool Paris store opened in Paris in 2002 by the former art director of Daft Punk. It's bright, white and elegant as an ice maiden but it's not so intimidating that you can't venture in. Staff are lovely, and the clothes are—well, they're expensive, but also irresistible. And don't even look at the leather bags, which are also covetable but eye-poppingly high in price. You may need a drink at the NoMad next door to recover. *1170 Broadway. www.kitsune.fr*

MARIMEKKO This Finnish brand is known for its colourful, graphic prints, and its new Flatiron store (the flagship boutique) is a fitting tribute to the famous brand. With windows that are always fun to look at (my favourite display was a fabric dinner party made out of Marimekko's best designs, complete with tiered fabric cake), and an interior that's a joy to walk around (as you would expect of this colourful company), this store is pulling in the fans. There are tablecloths, pillows, comforters and curtains, and if you can't find what you want the fabric can also be bought by the yard for some DIY. *200 Fifth Avenue. www.marimekko.com*

NEW YORK VINTAGE Another great store that adds to the charm of this neighbourhood, New York Vintage is renowned for its well-curated selection of pieces. Its specialty is vintage couture, and designer clothing and accessories, and its collection spans a century. Loved by stylists searching for the perfect red-carpet gowns for their celeb clients, it's also become a go-to for fashion peeps looking for something different to stand out in the New York crowd. (In this age of Instagram, you always have to be snap-ready.) And if you can't afford to buy, there's an enormous rental facility. *117 West 25th Street. www.newyorkvintage.com*

OPENING CEREMONY If you can't make it down to the smart NoLIta boutique of this much-talked-about label, then the Ace Hotel has a condensed collection in a cute little hotel gift store. Stocking the witty ephemera

TIPS FROM AN INSIDER

Winn Coslick
New York producer / screenwriter

While there are still galleries in SoHo, the center of the New York City art world has relocated to the neighborhood of **Chelsea**. After exploring the cutting edge, a great place to relax is the restaurant **Trestle on Tenth**: fantastic food, a charming garden, and one the most adventurous wine lists in town. *242 Tenth Avenue. www.trestleontenth.com*

One of the city's most overlooked parks is **Madison Square Park**, near the Flatiron Building. In addition to its fountains, flowers and statues, it's also right across

Fifth Avenue from **Eataly**, the Italian food market that buzzes with New Yorkers and European tourists alike. If you like incredibly fresh seafood, sit at Il Crudo where the oysters, razor clams, and live sea urchin (when available) are not to be missed.

If you decide to venture over to Brooklyn, don't forget to see what's going on at **BAM, the Brooklyn Academy of Music.** *30 Lafayette Avenue, Brooklyn. www.bam.org* Don't miss the **Brooklyn Botanic Garden either.** *1000 Washington Avenue, Brooklyn. www.bbg.org*

and edgy fashion that OC is known for, it's great if you're staying nearby and need a flash outfit, fast! *20 West 29th Street. www.openingceremony.us*

RESTORATION HARDWARE
Restoration Hardware has changed its image in recent years, and gone from an upmarket and highly respected but, well, sometimes unimaginative, home furnishings and hardware chain to one that's edgier, innovative and altogether more interesting. (One friend calls it 'the new Pottery Barn'.) An example of how the company has done an aesthetic turn-around is the magnificent new store in Boston, housed in an historic 1960s building. The interior is so beautiful it almost steals the show from the product. The company is renowned for its furniture and elegant homewares, but it's recently added what it calls 'objects of curiosity'—architectural fragments, Chinese porcelain dinnerware and items that look almost

museum-ish. The Flatiron store is a fantastic place to walk around and get design ideas for your home—although the prices are so reasonable, it's easy to contemplate buying a tufted sofa or an aged timber coffee table. (In line with its new look, the company has recently rebranded itself as RH, so look for signage to that effect.) *935 Broadway. www.restorationhardware.com*

WOLF HOME You know those glamorous swathes of silk taffeta curtains that hang in the (usually double-height) homes of the wealthy, the stylish and those who live in grand Haussmannian apartments in Paris? Well, Wolf Home is where you come if you want some of that drapery drama. This store specialises in spectacular silks and silk-blend fabrics, and offers both custom and pre-made draperies and pillows, bedding, furniture and accessories. (The silk pillows are sublime.) *936 Broadway. www.wolfhomeny.com*

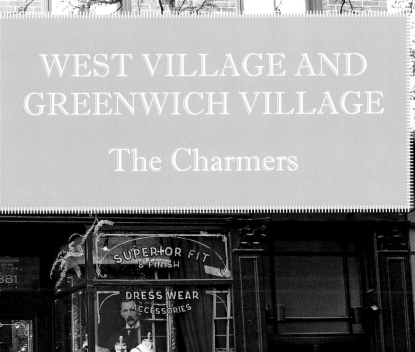

WEST VILLAGE AND GREENWICH VILLAGE

The Charmers

West Village & Greenwich Village

I regret profoundly that I was not an American and not born in Greenwich Village.
—John Lennon

Few New York neighbourhoods have been discussed, debated, extolled and eulogised as much as the charming enclave known simply as 'the Village'. Encompassing the West Village and Greenwich Village, it is possibly Manhattan's most loved corner. Which is why there is an audible collective gasp of horror whenever something about it changes. Locals in this part of town may be liberal-minded about sexuality, politics, culture and even fashion, but if something in their beloved hood is modernised, hipster-ised, or simply pulled aside to make way for something newer, shinier and more highly branded, they tend to be a little vocal about it. So, too, does the rest of New York. (The sight of big fashion brands such as Ralph Lauren and others moving into the old mom-and-pop stores has been fuelling media columns for years.) This is because the West Village and Greenwich Village epitomise 'old New York'. With their charming houses, cobblestoned streets and cute corner stores, these places are the two neighbourhoods many New Yorkers dream of living in. A friend calls them 'New York on a human scale'. You can see why locals don't want the area to change.

Of course, some lament that this once quaint, beatnik-y, bohemian artists' haven—the East Coast birthplace of the Beat movement—has changed through gentrification, and that it has subsequently become an expensive, upmarket faux-boho neighbourhood that only the wealthy can afford. (While there are still many galleries, cultural places and professional creatives around, most of the struggling artists that made this place famous have long fled. The only 'artists' who live here now are the successful actors, actresses, fashion designers, film directors and producers and big-name photographers, who can afford it.) However, the Village still retains the mood, philosophy, and indeed, aesthetic

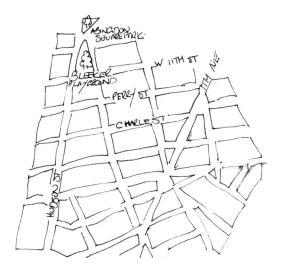

of those early boho days. As well as the Parisian-style cobblestoned streets (very Left Bank), lovely cafés, old brownstone homes, open-minded attitude, glorious artistic spirit and general joie de vivre, there is a gentle charm here that's rarely found in the rest of Manhattan.

The European feel also permeates the fashion and style. Businesses here are creative and innovative, but the shopfronts and buildings they're in retain the splendid dignity and often the gracious old interiors of the early days. It's an experience just to wander the streets.

As for street fashion, well anything goes. Locals like to stroll the streets in a mix of low-down vintage and high-end, haute-inspired pieces. That's the wonderful thing about this neighbourhood: the more imaginative you are, the more people applaud your efforts.

VILLAGE TRIVIA

In Alfred Hitchcock's 1954 film *Rear Window*, James Stewart's character lives in a Greenwich Village apartment. In the 1957 film *Funny Face*, Audrey Hepburn's character, Jo Stockton works at a bookstore in the Village, where she is discovered by Fred Astaire. And in Audrey's 1967 film *Wait Until Dark*, her character Susy Hendrix lives at 4 St Luke's Place.

In real life, the neighbourhood is home to *Vogue* editor Anna Wintour, Sarah Jessica Parker, Brooke Shields, Hugh Jackman, Julianne Moore and *Vanity Fair* editor Graydon Carter.

STAY: The new **Marlton Hotel** is a study in sublime design. Rooms are small but studded with charm, while the main hotel spaces are splendidly chic. *5 West 8th Street. www.marltonhotel.com.* Another gorgeous little hotel is **The Jade,** where the rather sexy décor is a modern take on 1920s jazz-age glamour. There's a cosy restaurant and adjoining lobby, which has a great little library and a lovely fire. *52 West 13th Street. www. thejadenyc.com*

BRUNCH: A casual but chic, French-style bistro is **Café Cluny**, where the interior design is so pretty bloggers are constantly photographing it. The food is delish, too. *284 West 12th Street. www.cafecluny.com.* Two further bistro treasures are **Joseph Leonard** *(170 Waverly Place; www. josephleonard.com)* and **Jeffrey's Grocery,** *(172 Waverly Place; jeffreysgrocery.com).* They sit opposite each other and have the same relaxed, effortlessly cool vibe. Sometimes there's a wait for a table, but the atmosphere inside each is worthwhile. And if you're British or Australian and you're missing the flavours of home, try **Tea & Sympathy.** Dubbing itself as 'a quintessential corner of England', it offers classic Anglo fare. Or simply a good old-fashioned cup of tea to pick you up. *108 Greenwich Avenue. www.teaandsympathynewyork.com*

DINE: Some argue that President Obama put **Blue Hill** on the map when he took Michelle there for a romantic dinner one night, but the truth is, it was famous way before the White House phoned for a booking. Blue Hill has been known for its fresh ingredients and creative ways with vegetables for years (its sister restaurant Blue Hill at Stone Barns grows much of the produce). A favourite dish with many dinners is Vegetables on a Fence: a genius way to display produce by presenting the humble vegetable like a still life on a rack. Foodies love the creativity. *75 Washington Place. www.bluehillfarm.com*

BROWSE: Three Lives & Company has been part of the landscape in the Village since 1978, and will hopefully continue to be so for decades to come. This iconic bookstore once received an award for being 'an island of civility'. The selection of books is always interesting but it is the staff who are the real literary treasures: full of great advice and recommendations. Curiously, they like to arrange books face-out, so on entering the store, customers are met with a fantastic mix of colour and subject matter—'it's just a pleasurable way to browse', says one staffer. The store also frequently hosts author readings. Author Michael Cunningham says he goes there to remind himself why he writes novels. *154 West 10th Street. www.threelives.com*

EXPLORE: Lomography Gallery Shop is a must for photographers. This delightful store was founded when two students discovered a small Russian camera in the 1990s. Since then, the duo have taken their Lomo obsession and created an entire retail concept around it, creating a store—and indeed a photographic community—devoted to Lomo photographs. There are lenses, and instructive and historical photo books, but most buyers are simply fascinated by the cameras. There are now stores all over the world but this, the original Lomography shop, has become renowned. *41 West 8th Street. www.lomography.com*

SIT: The gardens of **St Luke in the Fields** church are well hidden; the entrance is via a quiet iron gate on Hudson Street. Behind this gate and the high churchyard walls lies a lovely 2-acre labyrinthine garden of walkways, blooming flowerbeds (including roses, tulips, cornflowers and lilies), pretty cherry trees, lush borders, and quiet benches to sit and contemplate the wonder of Mother Nature while the city rushes by outside. If you want to talk about miracles, there are some horticultural ones right here. *487 Hudson Street. www.stlukeinthefields.org*

WANDER: Washington Square Park. Those of a certain generation will recognise the arch of Washington Square Park from the opening credits of the TV series *Friends* (Monica's apartment was set in Grove Street). Though the park is located in the middle of an affluent neighbourhood, it's famous for attracting an eclectic and often quirky mix of people, which makes for great entertainment on a sunny day. There is always something to see here, from buskers to people dressed up in costume to tuxedoed piano players tickling the ivories of a baby grand in the middle of the square. *Between Washington Square North and Washington Square South. www.nycgovparks.org/parks/ washingtonsquarepark*

From top left: The boutiques of the West Village have a deliberate old-time feel, while Cafe Cluny has a chic French vibe.

Opposite: Shopping ranges from big-name stores to small, eclectic boutiques.

West Village & Greenwich Village

FASHION, STYLE AND DESIGN DESTINATIONS

ABINGDON 12 A beautiful little store, and one many consider a West Village gem, this boutique is tucked into a pre–Civil War townhouse. It offers an interesting and well-curated collection of goods, ranging from modern to vintage objects (ornate doorknobs and antique jewellery), but its strength is its exclusive line of in-house stationery. Just charming. *613 Hudson Street.*

AEDES DE VENUSTAS Marie Antoinette would have adored this French-inspired delight of a store. It's opulent, luxurious and completely over the top, with gilded wallpaper, a fabulously grand chandelier and an antique desk as the checkout counter. It's also scented like a movie star's boudoir, with luxurious fragrances, candles, lotions and soaps from high-end brands like Diptyque and Annick Goutal, as well as cult labels like Aēsop, Astier de Villatte and Penhaligon's. Great for gifts, as well as indulgences for yourself. *9 Christopher Street. www.aedes.com*

ALBERTINE A lovely boutique that stocks both vintage and consignment clothing, plus exquisite fashion (including great indie labels), custom jewellery and other beautiful things, Albertine is a true surprise of a store. The wonderful staffers, alongside owner Kyung Lee, are matched by the impeccable collections that range from floaty, feminine fashion pieces to amazing jewellery—including delicate vintage pieces displayed in glass cases. The pink Louis XIV–style chairs and birdcages further add to the girly feel. There's also a bespoke dressmaking service, to further entice. *13 Christopher Street. www.albertine.co*

ALEXIS BITTAR The jewellery designer who started out selling his designs from a humble SoHo street stall now has three shops to his name: each selling his extraordinary designs handcrafted in his Brooklyn atelier. The choice pieces are the sculptural ones: perfect for pairing with a little black dress for that va-va-voom factor. *353 Bleecker Street. www.alexisbittar.com*

BOOKBOOK With its charming name (and yes, there's no space between the words) bookbook is one of those rare things: an independent bookstore that's still going strong. Shelves are elegantly designed and full of good reads, while staff leave you be to browse. Just perfect. *266 Bleecker Street. www.bookbooknyc.com*

CASTOR & POLLUX Previously based in Williamsburg, Kerrilyn Palmer's Castor & Pollux made the move to the West Village just a few years ago, but it seems right at home on the tree-lined street it occupies. The intimate store could belong in *Mad Men* with its elegant old displays, but its offerings are utterly modern. The boutique is a go-to for girls who eschew trends and favour feminine classics with a twist, such as Marais shoes, Risto Bimbiloski coats, Sonia Rykiel knits and Acne Jeans. *238 West 10th Street. www.castorandpolluxstore.com*

CO BIGELOW This atmospheric, 171-year-old pharmacy—the oldest apothecary in the United States—is full of equal parts product and history. Amid the charmingly old-fashioned space you can stumble across all kinds of hard-to-find beauty products, from European imports to CO Bigelow's own famous signature line. *414 6th Avenue. www.bigelowchemists.com*

CONSIDEROSITY West Village boutiques have the best names. This cutie is a great gift store, where the products really are well considered. This being the West Village, there are lots of gorgeous artisanal home goods and handmade jewellery, and most of them are unique. Great for picking up unusual treasures for daughters or friends. *191 West 4th Street.*

CYNTHIA ROWLEY This label has long been a wardrobe staple for the stylish New Yorker looking for some flirty fashion for those rooftop terrace parties. The tailored coats are eye-catching too—and take the dresses from day to evening with ease. *376 Bleecker Street. www.cynthiarowley.com*

EDON MANOR Okay, so it's a bit further south of the Village, but this is one seriously beautiful boutique that's worth the extra trek. Inspired and styled like an English country manor—albeit one that looks like it was designed by Dior—it features beautiful old books and green velvet wingbacks alongside stunning floral bouquets. In between all this English manor loveliness are shelves of equally pretty accessories. The shoes are particularly covetable but it's the pieces by Givenchy and Alaïa that really make shoppers go weak at the knees. *391 Greenwich Street. www.edonmanor.com*

FISCH FOR THE HIP Both this neighbourhood and the Flatiron/NoMad area are packed with secret vintage stores. This one has a surprisingly good collection, including a lot of lovely Hermès Birkins and Chanel tweed jackets. *33 Greenwich Avenue. www.fischforthehip.com*

MICK MARGO Named after the owner Nadine Feber's grandfather, who apparently was quite a dandy, Mick Margo is an ode to sartorial splendidness. Despite the moniker, it's a women's boutique, and the emphasis is firmly on femininity— French femininity to be exact. There are Repetto flats, pieces from the always-gorgeous collections of Isabel Marant, clothing by Cacharel, and even glamorous sunglasses from Karen Walker, in which super-blogger Blair Eadie from *Atlantic Pacific* always seems to be decked out. *19 Commerce Street. www.mickmargo.com*

MILLER'S OATH Like Edon Manor above, Miller's Oath is a little further south than the Village, but worth the stroll if you're into bespoke tailoring, and especially into beautiful bespoke shirts. It's the kind of place where you can be measured for a finely fitted, French-cuffed white shirt to impress the clients (or boss) at that next business meeting. Shirts and suits like this are worth the money, as fans of Savile Row will attest. *510 Greenwich Street. www. millersoath.com*

RAG & BONE It began as a line of denim clothing in 2002 but has since expanded to cover great pieces of every description for both men and women. The emphasis is on craftsmanship, and Rag & Bone really knows how to craft gorgeous stuff. Their jeans fit, while still making you look thin (or deliciously curvy), and even the sweaters will make you look like a model. Many buyers love the riding jackets (so flattering), which are traditionally cut while still looking chic and contemporary. The merchandising is similarly appealing: rugged furnishings, decorative vintage pieces and exposed brick walls. It's a look that's timeless, yet right on trend. (They have several stores in Manhattan.) *100–104 Christopher Street. www.rag-bone.com*

THE INK PAD This could be Manhattan's only store dedicated to rubber stamps and the paper arts, and if you're into stationery and creating your own wrapping and packaging, it's the perfect place to come. There are thousands of stamps, stencils and other things to customise your wrapping paper and greeting cards, or as some people are doing, pretty up a hessian shopping bag or canvas weekender. There are also craft punches and magazines like *Craft Stamper* for ideas. *37 7th Avenue. www.theinkpadnyc.com*

There are many more stores in the Village but I encourage you to explore the area for yourself, as there are far too many boutiques to include in just a few pages.

Tea&Sympathy

West 11th Street

Magnolia Bakery

Perry Street

Greenwich Avenue

Cynthia Rowley

Fisch for the Hip

Waverly Place

Charles Street

Alexis Bitter

CO Bigelow

Greenwich Street

Hudson Street

Bleecker Street

Three Lives & Company

West 10th Street

Aedes de Venustas
and Albertine

Jeffrey's Grocery

Christopher Street

The Marlton Hotel

Joseph Leonard

Church of St
Luke's in the Field

Considerosity

Waverly Place

Bedford Street

7th Avenue

West 4th Street

Blue Hill

Washington
Square Park

Avenue of the Americas

bookbook

West 4th Street

*Map is not to scale and not
all streets/places are shown.*

THE MEATPACKING DISTRICT AND CHELSEA

The Cool Kids

The Meatpacking District & Chelsea

A well-dressed woman offers a pair of gloves to a homeless person: *Sir, could you use these?*
Homeless person: *Lady, you should know better. Those don't match my outfit!*
—overheard in MePa

For a few years there in the late 1990s or early 2000s, the Meatpacking District (MePa) was a land living on the edge: a semi-industrial, rough-around-the-edges, slightly dangerous, come-if-you-dare kind of place. It was a dark neighbourhood frequented by the club crowd (who loved the seediness, and the dim bars and dance clubs), the gay crowd (always the first to recognise the next 'in' place), and the model-slash-photographer crowd. If you came here you were hip. Cool. And clearly in the know. New Yorkers searching for their next urban 'fix' (read: thrill) found it exhilarating, stimulating and enormously sexy (thanks in part to the club scene). It was somewhat ironic that an area that had started life as granite works, an iron foundry, and then a market selling meat and poultry had become one of Manhattan's most fashionable places, but nobody seemed to care. MePa was the place to be.

Then, the hype began to plateau as MePa's 'edge' wore off. Still people came, though, lured by the promise of a good time. Gallerists, designers, photographers, retailers and other creatives followed, colonising the neighbourhood and seeking secret lofts and warehouses to rent. (The Meatpacking District proper—a tiny trapezoid framed by Gansevoort Street, West 14th Street, Hudson Street and the West Side Piers—is not zoned for residences, so people live there illegally, in commercial buildings or tucked-away lofts, or else in adjacent streets like Horatio or Jane in the West Village.)

Sensing that it had staying power, entrepreneurs like Keith McNally opened bars and bistros. Alongside them, design-heavy hotels such as the Gansevoort and The Standard brought in the foreign travellers, eager to see what the fuss was about.

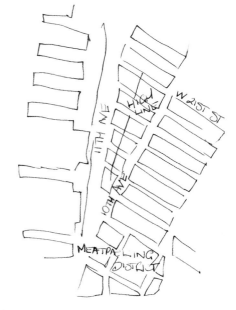

Today, this area is a bustling powerhouse of a place, populated by stunning bars and bistros, and amazing spaces carved out of rusty old lofts and warehouses. It's still is a frighteningly cool quarter, but the style/fashion and gay crowd is being diffused by different demographics, from business people to families. Some lament that MePa has lost its character, but others suggest the area could, thanks to additions like the High Line and the new Whitney Museum, continue to be one of the most vibrant, creative quarters of Manhattan. The shopping here is particularly good, and focuses on edgy new labels as much as high-end designers.

In neighbouring Chelsea, meanwhile, a similar story is being told. Although Chelsea was always slightly more upmarket than MePa, with many delightful streets, gorgeous townhouses and a village feel, it was still gritty in parts, and crime was a problem. Now, it has become gentler, even charming in places. Old buildings have been given a new lease of life—the former Nabisco factory now houses the Chelsea Market—and some locals feel Chelsea has become much like the Village (meaning Greenwich Village), just without the pretentious factor. If you're into art, Chelsea is the place to be, while the rest of the retail stores reflect the ethnic and social diversity of the area's population. In recent years, Chelsea has become an alternative shopping destination, with Barneys CO-OP, Comme des Garçons, and Balenciaga joining other newcomers like Alexander McQueen, Stella McCartney and Christian Louboutin. And if you love architecture, the Chelsea Historic District (from 20th Street to 22nd Street, between 8th Avenue and 10th Avenue) is a must-see, as it features glorious buildings from the 1800s.

STAY: A great hotel is the **Maritime Hotel** *(363 West 16th Street. www.themaritimehotel.com).* This cutie is a nautical-themed hotel with port-hole style windows and a cool, breezy vibe. The most popular part is La Bottega, the bistro, which is superb on summer nights when you're looking for somewhere to have drinks outside. If you want more of a 'scene', try the **Gansevoort** *(18 9th Avenue. www.gansevoorthotelgroup.com)* or **The Standard** *(848 Washington Street. www.standardhotels.com/high-line),* but both can be crazy with action.

DINE: Set under the High Line on Washington Street, **The Standard Grill** has a thriving outdoor dining scene. In fact, it can be a bit over the top with celebs and star-watchers, but the atmosphere is undeniable. *Details as above.*

DRINK: Inspired by the gin mix created during the prohibition-era 1920s when poor-quality alcohol was mixed with other flavourings to become more drinkable, **Bathtub Gin** mixes its gin and other spirits with all sorts of curious ingredients. The cocktails are inspired by original recipes, and it's all rather fun. *132 9th Avenue. www.bathtubginnyc.com*

GRAZE: To put it simply, **Chelsea Market** is a one-stop gastronomic playground. Okay, that may seem a mouthful, but this place really is a mouthful. There is so much to eat here, your mind—and taste buds—will be overwhelmed by the choice. It's the home of the Food Network, so there's always something going on (you can watch shows being filmed here), but if you want to eat, there's everything from fish markets to wine stalls. *75 9th Avenue. www.chelseamarket.com*

BE ENTERTAINED: Inspired by the shadowy atmosphere of film noir, **Sleep No More** is unlike anything you may have seen. It's a show (of sorts) set in a five-storey building called The McKittrick Hotel. Inside, the rooms are outfitted to look like a ballroom, children's bedrooms, a padded cell, an antiquated lunatic asylum, doctor's offices, a cemetery, taxidermist's menageries and, well, the strange list goes on. The actors wear wardrobes to suit, which can be as disconcerting as the rooms. Each 'play' is different, and—much like a theatre—there are good and bad ones. Happily, there's a rooftop bar should you need to discuss it all afterwards. Only in New York. *530 West 27th Street. www.sleepnomorenyc.com*

WANDER: The Museum at the Fashion Institute of Technology, or the FIT for short, is a college but it's also one of the most fashionable museums in New York City. This is because its in-house museum puts on some of the best fashion exhibitions outside of the Met and London's V&A. (Shows held in 2014 include 'Elegance in an Age of Crisis: Fashions of the 1930s' and 'Trendology.') There is also an amazing calendar of free programs and talks ('Dressing the Screen: Costume Design in Hollywood' is a recent example), but they tend to sell out quickly, so consult the website and book early if you're going to be in town. *227 West 27th Street. www.fitnyc.edu*

WANDER: The High Line walking trail is such a fabulous concept: an old railway line elevated above the city streets transformed into a park for New Yorkers. And to think it was marked for demolition before a group of community-minded residence decided to save it and convert it into a public park. Those people ought to be canonised. The best thing is sitting on the timber deckchairs, with the scent of the flowers all around, watching the sun set over the Hudson. *Gansevoort Street to West 34th Street. www.thehighline.org*

STAY: The High Line Hotel is a new and spectacular hotel housed in a nineteenth-century Gothic landmark building that was built as a dormitory for a seminary. The much-discussed design team of Roman and Williams preserved the Gothic-style architecture, including the incredible Refectory Hall and the serene exterior. The rooms are a tranquil retreat—just as they are when they were used for those living in the seminary—while the exterior is a clever mix of playful spaces and Zen-like corners of peace, with spots to read, have coffee, mooch about with your kids near the water feature or just enjoy the sun. *180 10th Avenue. www.thehighlinehotel.com*

FASHION, STYLE
AND DESIGN DESTINATIONS

BEYOND 7 One for the dramatic dressers, this showroom specialises in 'oh-my' outfits. Think sexy frocks from Issa (one of the Duchess of Cambridge's faves), spectacularly long pearl necklaces from Erickson Beamon (think Chanel, only cheaper), and gorgeous garb from Orla Kiely, Benjamin Cho, Elise Overland and others. It's all edgy but elegant. *601 West 27th Street.*

DARLING If you're after an ultra-feminine dress to wow New York with, this is the place to come. It's famous for its pretty frocks, and the choice is outstanding. There's even a downstairs area filled with vintage treasures. *1 Horatio Street. www.darlingnyc.com*

DIANE VON FURSTENBERG Still going strong after all these years, Diane von Furstenberg and her signature wrap DVF dresses are a staple of many a New Yorker's wardrobe (especially for those weekends in the Hamptons). However, all of her clothes are covetable. They're bright but still sophisticated, flattering but still sexy, and modern while being timeless classics. The store (her flagship)

is a ray of sartorial sunshine, too: colourful, chic and full of personality. *874 Washington Street. www.dvf.com*

IRIS SHOES If you're a shoe connoisseur, step in here. The prices may be on the high side but so are the designs. There are sublime shoes from the likes of Chloé, Michael Kors, Marc Jacobs, Nina Ricci, Jil Sander, Rochas, Paul Smith and John Galliano. Bliss. *827 Washington Street. www.irisnyc.com*

JEFFREY A much-lauded store, this chic boutique carries a fantastic array of clothing. All the best designers are here: Balenciaga, Bottega Veneta, Céline, Chanel, Christian Dior, Dries Van Noten, Giambattista Valli, Givenchy, Jason Wu, Lanvin, Marni, Martin Margiela, Prada, Proenza Schouler, Saint Laurent, Stella McCartney, Thakoon and Valentino, to name just some. (You can see why's it's lauded!) The service can be hit and miss but there's no doubt the labels are worth the pain. It can be expensive, but occasionally you can find something that won't make you cry at the cost. *449 West 14th Street. www.jeffreynewyork.com*

MARLENE WETHERELL If you can't afford Jeffrey, come here. Marlene carries superb vintage pieces from names like Yves Saint Laurent, Céline and Chanel. This hidden Chelsea vintage shop is truly a great little fashion find. *40 West 25th Street. www.marlenewetherell.com*

NEST INTERIORS Run by the husband-and-wife team of Lana Sexton and Henry Stozek, Nest features everything from one-of-a-kind creations by small, local artisans, to internationally sourced vintage treasures. They're especially fond (as they should be) of Chelsea photographers, so there are always great New York prints on offer. *172A 9th Avenue. www.nestinteriorsny.com*

PIPPIN Named after the owners' Cavalier King Charles spaniel, Pippin, this gorgeous store features beautiful vintage jewellery and even more irresistible homewares. The former is the domain of co-owner Stephen, a trained gemologist, while his wife looks after the furniture and home goods. Choose from antique eternity rings and 1940s costume pieces designed by Coco Chanel herself, plus superb vintage handbags. *112 West 17th Street. www.pippinvintage.com*

TEN THOUSAND THINGS Designers David Rees and Ron Anderson are the names behind this boutique, and their stunning jewellery creations alone are worth popping into the store for. *423 West 14th Street. www.tenthousandthingsnyc.com*

THEORY Like its name, Theory is simple and understated, offering quality basics that you'll love forever, from classic blazers to feminine pants. The stores are as elegant as the clothes: black concrete floors, grey walls and wood details. *40 Gansevoort Street. www.theory.com*

TRACY REESE Girls—of all ages—love the clothes here. They're sweet without being sugary, sexy without being ho-ish, and—most importantly—have enough va-va-voom without showing too much va-va-what-the? *641 Hudson Street. www.tracyreese.com*

TRINA TURK These clothes are imbued with colour and feel casual enough for the beach or weekend, but are still stylish enough for work. *67 Gansevoort Street. www.trinaturk.com/boutique/new-york*

The High Line

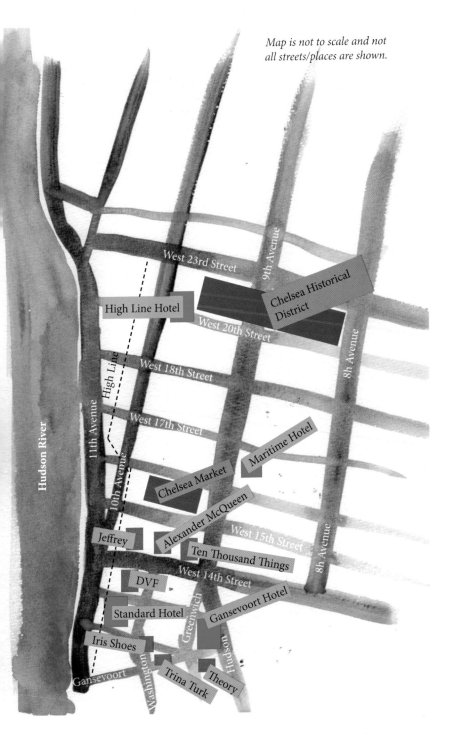

Map is not to scale and not all streets/places are shown.

Hudson River

West 23rd Street

9th Avenue

High Line Hotel

Chelsea Historical District

West 20th Street

High Line

West 18th Street

11th Avenue

8h Avenue

West 17th Street

10th Avenue

Maritime Hotel

Chelsea Market

Alexander McQueen

West 15th Street

Jeffrey

Ten Thousand Things

8h Avenue

West 14th Street

DVF

Standard Hotel

Gansevoort Hotel

Greenwich

Hudson

Iris Shoes

Washington

Gansevoort

Trina Turk

Theory

67

TRINA TUR

SLEEK + *Chic*

FALL

SOHO, LITTLE ITALY AND NOLITA

The Style Stalwarts

SoHo, Nolita & Little Italy

When I'm in New York, I just want to walk down the street and feel this thing, like I'm in a movie. —Ryan Adams

Oh, SoHo. What can we say that hasn't already been said a thousand times about this sassy, soignée and sometimes exasperating place? It's true that some people lament the changes—in both pace and population—that SoHo has undergone over the years, and the crowds are certainly maddening at time. However, others still feel passionate about this style stalwart. SoHo's the urban version of Linda Evangelista: a glamorous supermodel who still looks good after all these years, and who has both style and a don't-care attitude. It's strangely appealing. Venturing into SoHo (which stands for South of Houston Street, a major east–west thoroughfare in downtown Manhattan) is an exercise in bravery and bluff. You need to fake confidence to feel good when faced with all the startlingly gorgeous models and actresses in the lobby of the Mercer Hotel (where a great many of them go to talk deals with agents and producers about their next film, book or television show). And you need to have courage to walk into the designer stores and not flinch at the numbers on the price tags. The swarms of tourists can also be a pedestrian challenge:

if you're claustrophobic, don't go near the place on weekends, as the groundswells will drown you.

Despite these issues, SoHo is still one impressive place. This neighbourhood boasts the greatest collection of cast-iron architecture in the world, and its owners have thankfully preserved much of it. Most of the side streets also retain their endearingly wonky cobblestones. Sadly, many of the old artists' lofts have been turned into multimillion-dollar residences, but both the galleries and the artistic spirit are still there. (Even the optometrist has an extraordinary gallery wall of paintings and artwork, with which to test your vision.) Many of the stores sell unique and eclectic products, from upscale antiques and vintage furniture to eye-catching rugs, handbags, homewares and, of course, fashion. Most of the best boutiques and restaurants are clustered in the northern area of the neighbourhood, along Broadway and Prince and Spring streets; however, these sidewalks are often jammed with shoppers, tourists and annoyed locals. If you get off

the beaten tracks, you'll still discover great little stores and bistros, particularly around Elizabeth Street.

If you don't like crowds at all, or simply want to see boutiques that are a little different from the big, highly publicised brands, head for neighbouring NoLita (sometimes spelt NoLIta), which stands for 'North of Little Italy'. Once an Italian-centric enclave, it could almost be an Australian outpost now, thanks to the number of Aussies who live and work in the area, including supermodel Nicole Trunfio, a long-time resident. (A fair number of other celebrities live there, too, including David Bowie, Gabriel Byrne, Moby and John Mayer.) Yes, the postcard in this neighbourhood may be Manhattan but the mood is distinctly Aussie. Within both SoHo and the compact six-by-six-block territory of NoLIta, there are more than a dozen Australian boutiques and bars. In fact, if you hang around NoLIta's famous Mulberry Street for long enough, you'd swear by the accents that you were in Bondi, Sydney.

UNDERSTANDING NEIGHBOURHOOD NAMES

The name SoHo (sometimes referred to as Soho) refers to the phrase 'South of Houston' (Street). It was coined by urban planner Chester Rapkin, and spawned a new trend of renaming New York neighbourhoods with shorter, catchier acronyms. TriBeCa is short for 'Triangle Below Canal Street', NoHo is named for 'North of Houston Street', DUMBO is the cute moniker for 'Down Under the Manhattan Bridge Overpass', NoLIta is the nickname for 'North of Little Italy', and the new NoMad neighbourhood is named after 'North of Madison Square'. (There are many more, but sometimes they can become a bit silly. Even New Yorkers can't keep up with all the acronyms flying around.) Most of the terms eventually merge into general language use, and most are eventually spelt with all lowercase letters, almost as a mark of familiarity. You will see both spellings—the all-lowercase and a mix of upper and lower.

The Crosby Street Hotel
Opposite: Bond No. 9.

STAY: Crosby Street Hotel is one of the London-based Firmdale Hotels group's stylish swag of stay-aways. This New York outpost (its only overseas hotel, although others are in the works) is as colourful and as fashion conscious as the neighbourhood that surrounds it. Interiors are a joyous mix of colour, texture, fabrics and antiques, and rooms are all individually decorated in the same upbeat aesthetic. Or you could try **The Mondrian.** It doesn't get as much press as its neighbour, Crosby Street Hotel down the road, and that's a shame, because it's just as innovative and just as stylish. The exterior is a creative mix of conservatory-style elegance meets urban rusticity, while the greenhouse-inspired restaurant is truly one of the prettiest in town. (Keep an eye out for the glass cloches and the gardening tools lining the shelves—a nod to the greenhouse theme). The restaurant is a gorgeous place to come if you love gardens, but the rooms aren't shabby either. *Crosby Street Hotel: 79 Crosby Street. www.firmdalehotels.com; Mondrian: 9 Crosby Street. www.morganshotelgroup.com*

DINE: It's far from being a secret, but **Balthazar** still needs to be mentioned on any must-see list. This gorgeous French bistro has so much ambience it could teach its Parisian counterparts a thing or two! Sometimes it's difficult to get into for lunch, so try brunch or an early dinner. The people watching is as good as the interior design. *80 Spring Street.* *www.balthazarny.com*

WANDER: The lush, green $400-million **Hudson River Park** has transformed the riverfront landscape into the neighbourhood's longest, and perhaps most popular playground—at least in the daytime. It's not technically SoHo, but it's only a short wander from SoHo down West Houston, and the sea views and green spaces are a wonderful tonic to the downtown crowds on weekends. *59th Street South to Battery Park. www.hudsonriverpark.org*

BROWSE: Although many of the galleries that made SoHo a hot art hot spot in the 1970s and 1980s have decamped to Chelsea and the Lower East Side, there are still some excellent art spaces around, including **Peter Blum** and **Team Gallery**. (Team Gallery actually reversed the trend when it relocated here.) **Artists Space** is another worthwhile place to visit: it's one of the city's oldest alternative galleries and has helped to launch the careers of such art stars as Cindy Sherman. *Peter Blum: 20 West 57th Street. www.peterblumgallery.com; Team Gallery: 83 Grand Street. www.teamgal.com; Artists Space: 38 Greene Street. www.artistsspace.org*

SHOP: Le Labo is such a gorgeous store! No wonder people go on about it. The concept of two stylish French guys who moved to Manhattan from the scented village of Grasse in the south of France, Le Labo is set out like an old-fashioned science lab. The design encourages you to create your own custom-made scent, which is what this store is all about. All you need to do is think of your favourite smells (jasmine, summer, the sea and so on), and they'll help you configure a fragrance to suit your personality. Each perfume is customised to the client, so you can be sure that no-one else will be wearing your scent. *233 Elizabeth Street. www.lelabofragrances.com*

LE LABO
GRASSE – NEW YORK

The Mondrian Hotel

FASHION, STYLE
AND DESIGN DESTINATIONS

ALEXANDER WANG This was Wang's first retail outpost and is a fitting shell to show off his skills in fashion design. The austere, pared-back space is much like a gallery—and some feel it's a little cold—but it works because it shows off the clothes magnificently. Clothes as art? Mr Wang clearly thinks so. *103 Grand Street. www.alexanderwang.com*

AVAMARIA Owner Katherine Virketiene has an eye for a divine outfit—and a divine designer. Her boutique features some of Manhattan's most interesting up-and-coming designers. However, she's also fond of the luxe labels, and—unbelievably—isn't afraid to mark them down. In fact, her store has become well known for heavily marking down high-end designer labels (by up to 70 per cent), including those by Alberta Ferretti, Miu Miu and Stella McCartney. There are also sumptuous shoes by the likes of messieurs Manolo Blahnik and Jimmy Choo. *107 Crosby Street. www.virketyne.com*

BIT+PIECE Another retail darling for discount hunters, Bit+Piece is—much like its name—unconcerned with conventionality. Instead, it likes to mix

things up to create a fashion boutique that offers fantastically eclectic pieces—with (wait for this) most at 65 per cent off their original prices. Prepsters will adore the Ralph Lauren, Donna Karan and Max Mara, while hipsters will head straight for the faux-fur hoodies. There are also great classic pieces from Theory, gorgeous dresses from Woo, chic casual items from Three Dots and even covetable numbers from Helmut Lang. It's a small space but most of the labels are top quality. *246 Mott Street. www.bit-piece.com*

ERICA WEINER Erica Weiner's collection has attracted attention from jewellery lovers because her collections range from vintage to antique, all of them handmade in Manhattan. They make for a lovely memento to take home. *173 Elizabeth Street. www.ericaweiner.com*

THE EVOLUTION STORE New York (and Paris, for that matter) loves a bit of taxidermy, and this store fulfils collectors' fantasies. There's everything from the now-ubiquitous heads (seemingly found on every other restaurant wall in downtown New York), to less scary natural displays.

Quirky and interesting, even if you don't have anywhere to put them. *120 Spring Street. www.theevolutionstore.com*

HOUSING WORKS BOOKSTORE CAFE

This bookstore and café offers two levels of literary loveliness, ranging from the latest and greatest fiction to nonfiction, rare books and collectibles. All proceeds from the café go to providing support services for homeless people living with HIV/AIDS. The bookstore also hosts an impressive schedule of literary events. *126 Crosby Street. www.housingworks.org/bookstore*

INA Ina has long been a shopping haunt for in-the-know fashion folk. But then, so many 'insiders' started to come here for their wardrobes that word leaked out and now, well, it's not so secret. But the clothes are still spectacular. It specialises in second-hand designer wear and shoes, but the clothes here are far from dusty relics of another time. Think Balenciaga, Tom Ford and Yves Saint Laurent. And Ina knows her stuff. If you want something special, just ask: she may have just the right frock out back. *21 Prince Street. (Men's store at 19 Prince Street.) www.inanyc.com*

JONATHAN ADLER Jonathan Adler has built a reputation on colour. In fact, 'bold and bright' is firmly part of his design philosophy. His furniture and homeware pieces are reminiscent of Palm Beach in the golden days: cocktail shades and retro lines that are designed to make you smile. They're modern enough to sit comfortably in a contemporary living room, while still being a little nostalgic in style. His mantra is: 'your home should make you happy', and his collections do just that. *53 Greene Street. www.jonathanadler.com*

KIKI DE MONTPARNASSE Named after the seductive French icon and Man Ray muse, this sexy little store is lined with a lot of posh lingerie. Plus, er, other things that can be used in the same room. *79 Greene Street. www.kikidm.com*

KIRNA ZABÊTE A beautifully designed store, with painted floorboards and white walls, this boutique stocks pretty numbers by the likes of Balenciaga, Lanvin and Chloé, plus stylish art and fashion books for inspiration and/or further self-indulgence. *477 Broome Street. www.kirnazabete.com*

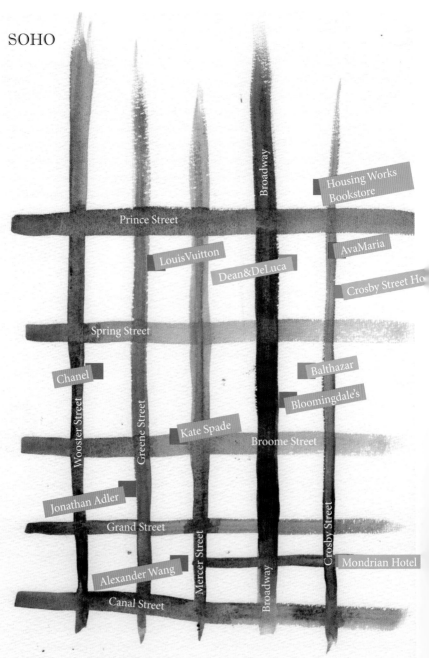

SOHO

Housing Works
Bookstore

AvaMaria

Crosby Street Ho

Prince Street

LouisVuitton

Dean&DeLuca

Spring Street

Chanel

Balthazar

Bloomingdale's

Wooster Street

Greene Street

Kate Spade

Broome Street

Jonathan Adler

Grand Street

Crosby Street

Mondrian Hotel

Alexander Wang

Mercer Street

Broadway

Broadway

Canal Street

*Maps are not to scale and not
all streets/places are shown.*

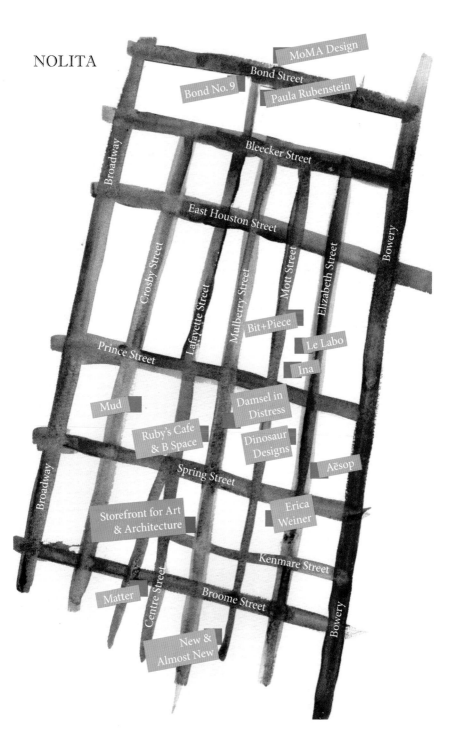

NOLITA

MoMA Design

Bond Street

Bond No. 9

Paula Rubenstein

Bleecker Street

Broadway

East Houston Street

Crosby Street

Lafayette Street

Mulberry Street

Mott Street

Elizabeth Street

Bowery

Bit+Piece

Le Labo

Ina

Prince Street

Mud

Damsel in Distress

Ruby's Cafe & B Space

Dinosaur Designs

Aësop

Spring Street

Broadway

Erica Weiner

Storefront for Art & Architecture

Kenmare Street

Centre Street

Matter

Broome Street

Bowery

New & Almost New

Kate Spade's colourful
SoHo store.

MATTER A great selection of international furniture, homewares and jewellery can be found here, including surprising pieces by star-architect Zaha Hadid. There are also New York–centric designs: great ideas for gifts. Some of the most beautiful are the miniature porcelain buildings by Johnathan Hopp. *405 Broome Street. www.mattermatters.com*

MOMA DESIGN STORE MoMA's design stores (there are several scattered around Manhattan) never disappoint. They always have quirky and cute things that make for great gifts, plus the more expensive, high-end design stuff, from vases to tech gadgets. *81 Spring Street. www.momastore.org*

OAK This is the perfect store for those who like their fashion simple, architectural and mostly black. It stocks lines like Pleasure Principle and Grey Ant, together with the store's in-house label. There's also a lower-priced offshoot, cleverly called A.Ok. The aesthetic, which is very New York, has been called 'dark luxe', and it perfectly suits the city's urban style. *28 Bond Street. www.oaknyc.com*

NEW AND ALMOST NEW While many consignment and re-sale stores stock clothes that have been 'gently worn', a lot of the merchandise at this boutique is brand new. Okay, there are some pre-loved numbers, but both 'new' and 'almost new' are treated with love and care by owner Maggie Chan. And the labels are the kind to go crazy for: Prada, Chanel and Hermès, with prices capped at around $600. Furthermore, Maggie knocks an additional 20 to 50 per cent off every month. *171A Mott Street. www.newandalmostnew.com*

NOTE: Bond Street is technically in NoHo, but we've included it in this section as it's on the edges of SoHo and Nolita's neighbourhoods, and you can easily do all of them in a day—and the adjacent Bowery too.

AUSTRALIAN SPACES IN NOLITA

AĒSOP Beauty brand Aēsop is everywhere now, but this store seems to fit beautifully into this neighbourhood. *232 Elizabeth Street. www.aesop.com*

B SPACE Opened by Pete Maiden, a former Rolling Stone magazine staffer from Sydney, B Space sits right alongside the iconic Ruby's and is the newest Aussie expat in town. It's a concept store-come-studio-come-showroom designed to showcase Australian culture, brands and lifestyle, and includes such things as Volley shoes, Mambo fashion, Ellery eyewear, and Driza-Bone jackets. *219C Mulberry Street. www.bspacenyc.com*

DAMSEL IN DISTRESS Exclusively stocks Australian brands, such as Sass & Bide, Maurie & Eve and One Teaspoon. *236 Mulberry Street.*

DINOSAUR DESIGNS Exciting expansion into Manhattan from the highly recognisable jewellery brand, known for their gorgeous resin, silver and glass bracelets, and chunky necklaces. *211 Elizabeth Street. www.dinosaurdesigns.com.au*

MUD A great name for a great brand that specialises in beautiful, simple plates, bowls and other elegantly minimalist vessels. *91 Crosby Street. www.mudaustralia.com*

ZIMMERMANN A New York outpost of the stylish Australian fashion label, famous for sexy, high-luxe dresses and swoon-worthy beachwear. *55 Mercer Street. www.zimmermannwear.com*

OPENING CEREMONY Opening Ceremony has been packing them into its now-iconic Howard Street store for several years now. In fact, it's become something of a SoHo mecca for many fans. The appeal is the mix of both established brands (including those from other countries) and Opening Ceremony's own label, plus collaborations with creative souls like Chlöe Sevigny. *35 Howard Street. www.openingceremony.us*

PAULA RUBENSTEIN For many stylists, this is one of their favourite New York stores; a veritable treasure trove of design treats. Paula has one of the best eyes in the biz, and travels the world sourcing her goods. There's everything from gorgeous vintage fabrics to old apothecary bottles, whimsical ladders, mannequins, armoires, stools and other ephemera. It's a true wunderkammer of a place. You'll wander in and still be there, half an hour later, trying not to buy quirky antiques and wonderful fabrics that you've fallen utterly in love with. Paula herself is often in the store, and is a delight to speak with. *21 Bond Street. www.paularubenstein.com*

WHAT GOES AROUND COMES AROUND A much-loved vintage destination, where collections change constantly based on what's in fashion. (The owner can spot a new trend a mile away.) Pieces range from ornate, Gilded Age stuff, to covetable Chanel chains. *351 West Broadway. www.whatgoesaroundnyc.com*

Shopping in SoHo and nearby Bowery
offers all kinds of bright surprises,
from bold bedding at Jonathan Adler to
stunning quilts at John Derian.

John Derian.
Opposite: Schiller's.

BOWERY, EAST VILLAGE AND LOWER EAST SIDE

The Rising Stars

Bowery, East Village & Lower East Side

. . . .

Everybody ought to have a lower East Side in their life.—Irving Berlin

Of all the villages and neighbourhoods in Manhattan, the Bowery and the East Village are two of the most riveting—and possibly also two of the most talked about in the media. There's good reason for all this attention; you see, this part of Manhattan was once the archetype of a dangerous New York neighbourhood. It was the bad boy of Manhattan: unruly, unkempt and utterly nonconformist, but with surprising musical, literary and artistic abilities. (Those who have lived there include Allen Ginsberg, William S. Burroughs, Charlie Parker, Lenny Bruce, Willem de Kooning, Jean-Michel Basquiat, Robert Mapplethorpe, Iggy Pop, Patti Smith and Debbie Harry.)

Then—like another former renegade from New York, Mr Jay-Z—it grew up, shrugged off its bad boy image, left its troubled youth behind and focused on its talent, and its future.

Today, it not only gives off a completely different vibe, it also attracts a far different crowd. In fact, like Jay-Z, it's become a bit of a rock star.

The transformation of the East Village, and the Bowery within it, began with places like the Bowery Bar and The Bowery Hotel, as well as stores like John Derian. Retail and hotel destinations such as these were so cool they attracted people who wouldn't have otherwise ventured to this part of the city. The shift in spirit then moved below Houston Street with the opening of the New Museum in 2007, and hip bars and restaurants like Freemans on Chrystie Street. Having come for the nightlife, people soon fell in love with the area. It was slightly gritty and still had some of the 'old New York' feel about it, while still offering a slew of cool and sometimes even swanky new hangouts.

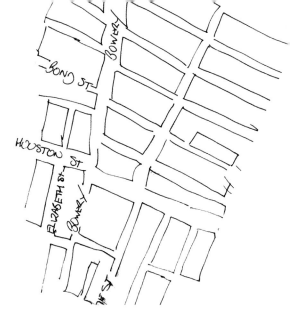

Fortunately, the rapid gentrification hasn't dulled the distinct character and personality of the place. There were always atmospheric places to drink; these have been simply joined by even more atmospheric little drinking holes, plus a great many gorgeous restaurants and cafés, amazing little quirky boutiques, and a handful of unusual galleries and hotels, all setting up shop to cater for the new generation of newcomers. In fact, this area has evolved into a mini retail mecca for everything indie and/or under the radar.

The thing about the Bowery, the East Village and the Lower East Side, is you never know what you'll find. Indeed, you probably won't find these retail experiences anywhere else. It also offers an interesting place to stroll around. One moment you could be walking along a retail street, trying to make up your mind whether you like or loathe the gritty landscape and late-night revellers spilling out onto the sidewalk looking for a hangover remedy; then, you'll turn down a residential street and the mood will change completely. There'll be beautiful old homes, kids playing in sprinklers in the middle of the road (clearly the traffic slow for them in respect), locals sitting on front stoops (steps) chatting in the sun, and dogs wagging their tales with delight to be part of such a convivial scene.

The Bowery and the East Village are landscapes of dark and light, of day and night, and of the working class and the highly successful living side by side. Some people love it here; others can't see what all the fuss is about. One thing's for sure about life on this side of Manhattan life: it is never boring!

STAY: The owners of the **Bowery Hotel** say that it's part museum and part hotel. You can certainly see the history and crafts-manship of this unique building when you check in. The rooms combine original touches (wood-beamed ceilings) with modern amenities (marble soaking baths), while the downstairs Gemma Restaurant is a cute, cosy place for a casual meal. Some guests love it so much they check in and stay for a year. *335 Bowery. www.theboweryhotel.com*

BRUNCH: **Katz's Delicatessen** was made famous as the setting for the orgasm scene in the Meg Ryan film *When Harry Met Sally*, and fans of the film still visit here for that reason. *205 East Houston Street. www. katzsdelicatessen.com*

DINE: **The General** is one of the hot new restaurants on Bowery, where top-chef winner Hung Huynh pulls out amazing dishes night after night, and the dining room is often packed with celebrities who are serious about food. The General's staffers are also very generous: chefs often cook and serve meals to the homeless in their kitchen. *199 Bowery. www.emmgrp.com/restaurants/the-general*

SNACK: Don't miss a dish at David Chang's popular noodle shop, **Momofuku Noodle Bar**. Or if you're an Aussie far from home or a local looking for a real 'ocker' taste, try **The Tuck Shop**. A tuckshop, for those not quite familiar with the term, is a quaint slang phrase for the school cafeteria. This cute bistro offers a lot more than the ol' school caf, but the Australian flavours are the same. The menu includes Chook Pie, traditional meat pies and even Australian beer. If you're Scandinavian, or love smoked salmon and other fish in all its forms, then the famous mini food emporium **Russ and Daughters** is your place. Russ and Daughters has been serving salmon, herring and other specialty goodies since 1914. Their sandwiches are particularly fantastic—and great for lunch on the go as you're wandering around this intriguing neighbourhood. *Momofuku: 171 1st Avenue. www. momofuku.com/new-york/noodle-bar; Tuck Shop: 68 East 1st Street. www.tuckshopnyc. com; Russ and Daughters: 179 East Houston Street. www.russanddaughters.com*

WANDER: While not exactly 'new', the **New Museum** is certainly one of the city's leading destinations for new art and new ideas. Designed by the Tokyo-based architect team of Kazuyo Sejima and Ryue Nishizawa/SANAA, it's a seven-storey, eight-level structure that is Manhattan's only dedicated contemporary art museum (hard to believe). Since it opened, it has become respected internationally for the adventurousness of its exhibitions, and has helped to draw lots of other cultural spaces to the LES. The **Tenement Museum** is another New York treasure, keeping alive the history of those who lived here decades ago via a series of restored apartments belonging to past residents at different time periods. *New Museum: 235 Bowery. www.newmuseum. org; Tenement Museum: 103 Orchard. www. tenement.org*

STROLL: St Mark's Place. One of the neighbourhood's most famous streets, this intriguing strip is lined with bars, restaurants and shops, and is a popular strip for tourists to visit. *East 8th Street.*

ARCHITECTURAL TRAIL TO TAKE: If you head along Stuyvesant Street towards 3rd Avenue, you'll find yourself wandering along one of Manhattan's prettiest blocks. The neighbourhood here is lined with nineteenth-century homes designed by architect James Renwick Jr. It's a delightful place, especially on a summer's afternoon.

Bowery Hotel

EXPLORE: Tompkins Square Park.
The East Village is a perfect example of how New York has villages within villages within villages. Within the East Village there is another vibrant micro-community called Alphabet City (actually, it's not that micro, since it comprises two-thirds of the East Village). Its name comes from avenues A, B, C and D, the only avenues in Manhattan to have single-letter names. It's a great place to wander around, at least during the day, but the really entertaining part is the 10.5-acre Tompkins Square Park. This is the recreational and geographic heart of the East Village, and has been the site of a lot of protests and riots over the decades. Now, it's a peaceful slice of greenery amid the urban landscape. The dog run—the first in New York City—is particularly fun to watch. It's almost a social scene unto itself, with the dogs left to play while their owners chat each other up on the side. *Between East 10th Street, Avenue B, East 7th Street and Avenue A. www.nycgovparks.org/parks/ tompkinssquarepark*

FASHION, STYLE
AND DESIGN DESTINATIONS

CLOAK & DAGGER If you love vintage clothing as much as new collections, as whimsy as much as practicality, this store's for you. It carries both the gorgeous vintage stuff and the glamorous new ranges, although its new ranges may just win you over more. With sunglasses from Karen Walker, Hollywod–style bathing suits from Seafolly and fantastic gift cards, it's a great place to source pretty things. There's another store in Brooklyn, too. *441 East 9th Street. www.cloakanddaggernyc.com*

DAGNY + BARSTOW A relative newbie in this neighbourhood, Dagny + Barstow has immediately become a popular place for up-and-coming designers as well as established contemporary brands. Labels include Margaux Lonnberg, Marcel, Dusen Dusen, Au Jour Le Jour and Mother of Pearl along with such stalwarts at Levi's. *264 Bowery. www.dagnyandbarstow.com*

EAST VILLAGE BOOKS This store has that slightly dishevelled, slightly cluttered but well-loved look that all good bookshops have. There are new titles as well as second-hand copies available, and there's always something interesting in the featured selection of art and photography. It's the kind of place where you never know what you'll find. *99 St Mark's Place. www.buyusedbooksnewyork.com*

DOYLE & DOYLE One of Manhattan's most loved antique and vintage jewellery stores, this goldmine is managed by sisters Elizabeth and Pamela Doyle (hence the name). Both have amazing taste in baubles, and as such their store is stocked with stunning jewellery pieces. It's particularly famous for its engagement rings: affordable and gorgeous. *412 West 13th Street. www.doyledoyle.com*

FABULOUS FANNY'S If you're in need of a new and preferably eye-catching pair of glasses, this is the place. Fanny's specialises in one-of-a-kind glasses, from Chanel-meets-Jackie-O numbers, to retro-inspired shades. The best pieces are the antique and vintage glasses. Furthermore, they start at reasonable prices. *335 East 9th Street. www.fabulousfannys.com*

GABAY'S Run by one family, this great little place sources its stock from the surplus that comes out of upmarket department stores. You may think that the concept doesn't warrant a look, but when you hear that the labels include the likes of Yves Saint Laurent, Marc Jacobs and Chanel, and that the prices are 50–80 per cent less than the originals … well, now you're interested, aren't you? So, too, are Gabay's regular buyers, who come here to snap up some CC action for their cocktail part-ees. You have to be persistent to find the beautiful bargains, but they are there. *225 1st Avenue. www.gabaysoutlet.com*

GARGYLE A mix between Brooks Brothers and Ralph Lauren, this label was inspired by early country clubs. It's preppy but also quite classic. There are various labels, and the store also has its own signature line. *16A Orchard Street. www.gargyle.com*

JOHN DERIAN COMPANY John Derian's store is like those wonderful, old-fashioned general stores that have long since disappeared. I suspect the 'look' is deliberate.

Full of trestle tables loaded with whimsical things, from Derian's famous decoupage plates (the ones with botanical prints are beautiful) to quirky vintage finds, it's a place to linger for ages. The adjacent stores, including his Dry Goods shop (a quirky play on words to reflect the 'general store' theme), are also Derian's, and feature more covetable collections, including beautiful vintage linens, delicately printed pillowcases and quilts. *6 East 2nd Street. www.johnderian.com*

OBSCURA ANTIQUES AND ODDITIES This East Village treasure has recently moved into a space that was once a funeral home. Macabre? Not at all, when you see the whimsical and wondrously freaky things it stocks. Famous for its antiques and rare taxidermy, Obscura feels a little like an old museum in Paris, full of artefacts and odd things that are strange and unusual. Owners Mike Zohn and Evan Michelson have such a good eye for curious pieces that the Discovery Channel gave them their own show, called *Oddities. 207 Avenue A. www.obscuraantiques.com*

Freeman's Sporting Club: a boutique ('sutlery') and barber in one.

HAND
TAILORED
CLOTHING

BARBER
SHOP

SUTLERY

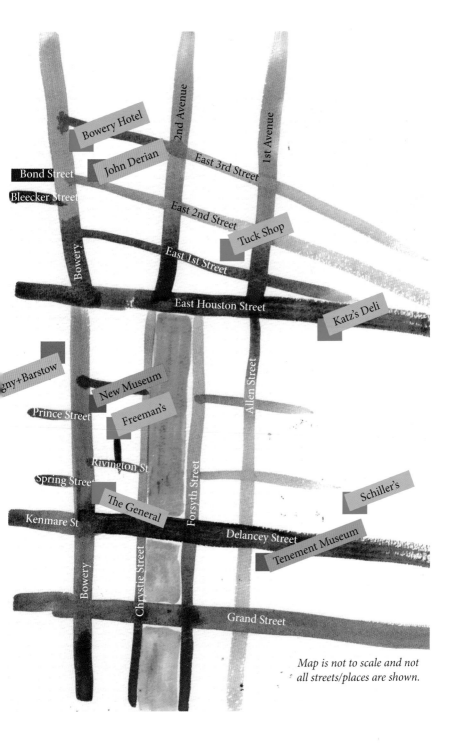

Map is not to scale and not all streets/places are shown.

PAS DE DEUX After the success of their men's store Odin, fashionable fellas (and friends) Eddy Chai and Paul Birardi decided to venture into women's clothing, which looks like being just as successful. Modelled after a Parisian boudoir, this charming store stocks a lot of great labels, from Rag & Bone to Comme des Garçons. *328 East 11th Street. www.pasdedeuxny.com*

ST MARK'S BOOKSHOP Along with the nearby Strand bookstore, St Mark's Bookshop is an East Village institution—and has been since the mid 1970s. Many of its customers are NYU students looking for academic texts, but there are also a lot of browsers who love coming here to flick through the art and design titles, and contemporary fiction. The selection is always eclectic, which is what helps to keep this place interesting—and in business. *31 3rd Avenue. www.stmarksbookshop.com*

SHOP: The idea of an enormous, no-frills, decorated-on-a-dime, 55 000 square foot bookstore, **Strand Books**, may not sound immediately appealing, and it sure doesn't look like an Assouline or Taschen bookstore when you walk in the door. But persevere, because the beauty of this place is in the discovery. The Strand not only houses thousands of new titles—and most of them discounted (in fact, I buy my Taschen here because they're much cheaper)—but also thousands upon thousands of used titles, including hard-to-find art, design, fashion and photography books. Upstairs, on the top floor, there are even more goodies in the form of rare books. It's still one of the best bookstores in New York. Recent discoveries have unearthed out-of-print Cecil Beatons, a vintage *In Vogue* for $20 and Bill Blass' autobiography *Bare Blass* for $5. Kate Spade's buyers reportedly come here for the vintage books displayed in Kate Spade stores. *828 Broadway. www.strandbooks.com*

BROOKLYN

The Creatives

A lot of my friends who grew up in Manhattan have a strange phobia about Brooklyn. It's big and scary and they get lost.—Moby

Brooklyn is the wild card of New York City. It's the unpredictable—and unexpectedly talented—outsider that swoops in and shows the rest how it's done. You could say it is the Kate Moss of New York: confident, uncompromising, unconventional and completely, utterly cool.

Brooklyn dresses to its own distinct style, decorates its houses to its own distinct aesthetic (equal parts retro and boho, with a splash of quirkiness), and its restaurants seem to run by the philosophy of 'anything goes'. Furthermore, its residents are an easy-going mix of creatives, corporates, students, successful professionals, newcomers and those who have lived there for generations. All of this combines to make Brooklyn one thoroughly captivating hood.

The problem that Brooklyn has now is its popularity, particularly the neighbourhood of Williamsburg ('Billyburg' to New Yorkers). Over the past few years, hundreds of thousands of hangers-on have headed across the bridge to discover B-Land, craning their Aviator sunglasses at the beautiful old brownstone houses to see what all the fuss is about. Add to this the fact that a lot of hipsters have recently moved in (think boys in plaid flannel shirts with beards and vintage work boots, and girls in vintage frocks riding cruiser bikes), and Brooklyn seems to have to died a small death from the weight of its newfound fame. Some lament that the 'authenticity' of the place has now gone.

But Brooklyn's originality is still there, underneath the headlines and the head-shaking cynics. There are artisans galore making incredible products and businesses, there are fantastic rooftop gardens that manufacture as much as a small farm,

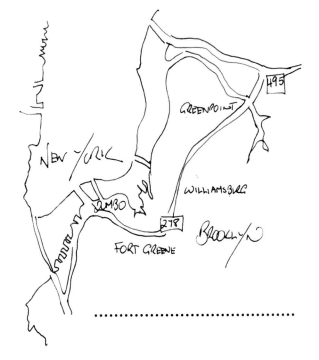

there are amazing bars, bistros, restaurants and streets full of architecture to explore, and yes, there are great vintage stores, too. You can take classes in chicken raising, rooftop gardening and cardboard furniture making. You can also barter books for wine, beer or tea at Molasses Books in Bushwick, a used bookstore that has made a business out of the Brooklyn barter system. Brooklyn is so egalitarian that you could grow a moustache or sideburns, heck you could walk around with unshaved legs, and nobody would raise an eyebrow.

But the most interesting thing about Brooklyn is its creativity. The place is a concentration of amazing imaginations. Culture, too, is big here. Some of the institutions include the Brooklyn Academy of Music (BAM), which includes a 2109-seat opera house, a 874-seat theatre, and an art house cinema; the Brooklyn Children's Museum; the Brooklyn Botanic Gardens; and New York City's second-largest public art gallery, the Brooklyn Museum.

Many visitors to New York overlook Brooklyn, because they believe that there's too much to see on the island of Manhattan itself, and it's too difficult to reach. Well, Manhattan does have a lot going on, but it would be a shame not to see and experience the eclectic charm that lies just across the bridges. Here are a few great places to begin your Brooklyn experience.

STAY: Ever since it opened, the **Wythe Hotel** has been a hit, mostly for its views of the New York skyline, but also for its atmosphere and its food—the rooftop bar (The Ides Bar) is one of the best places for a cocktail. And if you want a getaway, the rooms are inspiring, too. *80 Wythe Avenue. www.wythehotel.com*

DRINK: The name's confusing (it's set on Brooklyn's Manhattan Avenue), and its reputation may precede it, but the **Manhattan Inn** is still a good night out. It seems like a simple piano bar and restaurant designed in that salvage-heavy aesthetic that Brooklynites love (complete with bucket-seat banquettes and a farm-to-table menu), but when evening comes the atmosphere starts a-jumping. The piano is used to entertain during weeknights, but on weekends it's pushed aside to make room for the DJs, who mix up dance numbers to create a sweaty good time. It's the kind of place where everyone's friendly—and perhaps little drunk—and, well, you put the two together. It can be scene-y (lots of musos and models go), but in a nice way. *632 Manhattan Avenue. www.themanhattaninn.com*

DINE: If you can nab a reservation (tip: book a few weeks ahead), **Chef's Table** at **Brooklyn Fare is** the place to come for Brooklyn's best fare. With three Michelin stars, César Ramirez's restaurant in Boerum Hill specialises in spectacularly prepared seafood. The interior is austere because the focus is supposed to be on the dishes—and you will be amazed when they come out. *200 Schermerhorn Street. www.brooklynfare.com*

SNACK: Mast Brothers Chocolate is amazing! From the fabulous packaging (designers blog about Mast's beautifully printed, book-inspired ornamental wrappers) to the incredible flavours, Mast's choccy bars are as scrumptious as any in Willy Wonka's factory. Founded and run by two brothers in a former Williamsburg spice warehouse (the factory is open for tours), Mast offers chocolate you won't find anywhere else in the world. The brothers are so serious about their chocolate that they sailed nearly 20 tonnes of organic cacao beans on their own retrofitted, three-masted shipping schooner on a fifteen-day voyage from the Dominican Republic to Brooklyn, just to ensure it arrived safely. That's dedication to your craft. *111 North 3rd Street. www.mastbrothers.com*

WANDER: The **Brooklyn Botanic Garden** is one of New York's prettiest green spaces, even in the midst of a snowy winter (the camellias look magnificent against the snow). The Cherry Esplanade is lovely in April when the blossoms are out, while the Fragrance Garden shows you how a garden can charm with its scent as well as its sights. There's also a gorgeous perennial area, and a beautiful rose garden—a must-see in the summer months when tens of thousands of blossoms cascade down arches, climb up lattices, clamber over the pavilion, and pose in formal beds. *990 Washington Avenue. www.bbg.org*

Brooklyn

FASHION, STYLE
AND DESIGN DESTINATIONS

A&G MERCH Lots of fab furniture and unique objects, mostly in the modern vein, but all gorgeous. Manhattan dwellers happily go to Brooklyn just for this store. They also ship worldwide, if you live overseas. *111 North 6th Street. www.aandgmerch.com*

BEACON'S CLOSET This place can feel like your rich aunt's walk-in closet—after she's neglected it for twenty years. It's a little Miss Havisham-esque in atmosphere (lost in time), but that just makes it all the more exciting. You'll end up spending an hour or more rifling through the racks and layers, but don't think it's all dusty mess of uninspiring outfits. On the contrary, because the store is in Brooklyn's most stylish neighbourhood, this is where fashion insiders (editors, stylists and models) unload their unwanted clothes, so you're liable to find anything from a Diane von Furstenberg classic wrap to Levi's denims. *74 Guernsey Street. www.beaconscloset.com*

BIRD A delightful little boutique, Bird stocks equally delightful labels like Isabel Marant and Comme des Garçons. There are outposts in Cobble Hill and Park Slope, but the Williamsburg store is perhaps the prettiest. *203 Grand Street. www.shopbird.com*

BOOKCOURT A lovely, family-run independent bookstore with a well-curated selection of titles. Their fiction choices are particularly interesting. The store also holds regular readings by leading literary stars. *163 Court Street. www.bookcourt.com*

BROOKLYN FLEA People rave about this place, and the hype is justified. It's an enormous market where vendors from Brooklyn and beyond sell antiques, handmade/artisanal products (the food is fabulous) and other specialty things. On Saturdays, it's held at a lot in Fort Greene (176 Lafayette Avenue), and on Sundays it's at the Williamsburg waterfront (27 North 6th Street). In the winter (from Thanksgiving in November until March) it's moved inside at historic One Hanson (also known as the Williamsburg Savings Bank, at 80 North 5th Street), a fittingly grand place in which to stage it. *www.brooklynflea.com*

CATBIRD A teeny, tiny store, Catbird sells exquisite jewellery, ranging from classic pearls to contemporary pieces. *219 Bedford Avenue. www.catbirdnyc.com*

CITY FOUNDRY A mid-century fan's dream, this furniture store is stacked with fabulous furniture and accessories, and is beloved by designers and architects. *365 Atlantic Avenue. www.cityfoundry.com*

DALAGA An ultra-feminine shop where the emphasis truly is on the pretty, the frilly and the flirtatious. This sweet store stocks ruffled tops and dresses, colourful shoes and cute jewellery, all fabulously affordable (dresses start at $70; tops at $40). *150 Franklin Street. www.dalaganyc.com*

ERIE BASIN If you're one of those who've become obsessed by vintage and antique jewellery (there's a craze going down at present, much of it led by the new Great Gatsby film and the vintage Chanel necklace trend), then you had better head for this store. There are extraordinary antique, vintage and period pieces, from Art Deco engagement rings to Victorian mourning brooches. (Brooches are also very 'in' at the moment, thanks to Chanel.) This store alone is well worth the trip across the bridge. *388 Van Brunt Street. www.eriebasin.com*

FOXY & WINSTON Pretty and whimsical stationery by British-born illustrator Jane Buck. Just charming. *392 Van Brunt Street. www.foxyandwinston.com*

FRENCH GARMENT CLEANERS CO. Named after the dry cleaner who occupied the space in the 1960s, this Fort Greene boutique offers high-end fashion for women and men. *85 Lafayette Avenue. www.frenchgarmentcleaners.com*

ZOË Found inside a huge warehouse space in DUMBO, this place carries labels like Céline and Proenza Schouler. Just part of the contrasts for which Brooklyn is famous. *68 Washington Street. www.shopzoeonline.com*

CAFFÈ
STORICO

at the New-York Historical Society

170 CENTRAL PARK WEST · NY · NY · 10024

212.485.9211 · CAFFESTORICO.COM

G P H

GRAMERCY PARK HOTEL

TOP OF THE RO
OBSERVATION DE
at Rockefeller Center

GUEST: 1 AD
DATE: OCTOBER 19, 2
ENTRY TIME: 5:05 PM-5:20

16498114180557

SEQ No
8

Na
W
Ca

QANTAS
From

SYDNEY
Terminal 1

Service Information

ET

Gate

qantas.com

G P H

GRAMERCY PARK HOTEL

*Gramercy Park Hotel is the only commercial
building holding keys to Gramercy Park, the only
remaining private park in Manhattan.*

Have a pleasant evening and sweet dreams.
Thank you for staying at the Gramercy Park Hotel.

Tomorrow's high will be __79__ ° with a forecast of

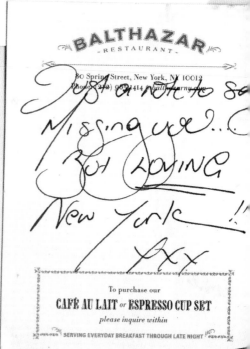

Flight	Date
QF 107	10SEP
	Seat

RK
7

NS
TA

67C

ding Time

915

Class

ECONOMY

INDEX

ACKNOWLEDGEMENTS

This book is the result of the wonderful, highly talented and extremely hardworking team at MUP, and I would like to sincerely thank them for not only commissioning it but also working on it with such care, love and attention to detail. I'm so grateful to be working with such a lovely team. Thank you to publisher Colette Vella, editor Penelope White, designer Emilia Toia, and the meticulous indexer Fay Donlevy. Thanks should also go to the production teams at Bookhouse and Splitting Image. Most of all, our heartfelt thanks go to you, the reader, for buying it. We hope it has given you lots of ideas and inspiration, and that you have a wonderful time visiting New York.

Six East Second Street New York NY 10003 (P) 212.677.3917 (F) 212.677.7197
www.johnderian.com

Argosy Book Store
Old & Rare Books
Established 1925

116 East 59th Street
New York, NY 10022

Tel 212-753-4455
Fax 212-593-4784

argosy@argosybooks.com   www.argosybooks.com

Architectural and Altered Antiques
www.oldegoodthings.com
mail@oldegoodthings.com

But God commends His love to us in that we being
yet sinners, Christ died on behalf of us. Rom. 5:8

PAULA RUBENSTEIN LTD.

21 Bond St.
New York, New York 10012

paula@paularubenstein.com   tel 212 966 8954